MARÍA JOSÉ ADROGUÉ

Education and disability
Diagnosis and proposals
for an inclusive school

Translation:
Rebeca O. Resnik
Mariano E. Jiménez

Adrogué, María José
Education and disability : Diagnosis and proposals for an inclusive school/ María José Adrogué. - 1a ed. - Rosario : Ediciones Logos Ar, 2022.

Libro digital, EPUB
Archivo Digital: online
Traducción de: Rebeca O. Resnik ; Mariano E. Jiménez.

ISBN 9798328678803

1. Inclusión Escolar. I. Resnik, Rebeca O., trad. II. Jiménez, Mariano E., trad. III. Título.
CDD 371.9046

*To my parents, role models and source of inspiration.
To my husband, without whose support and enthusiasm
nothing would be possible.
To my children, my four treasures.*

"Justice does not consist in giving to each one his due according to what is established and ordained, but above all in giving to each one that of which he is deprived or bereft and which corresponds to him according to a radically right order."

José Ramón Amor Pan
Ética y discapacidad intelectual

CONTENT

ABOUT THE AUTHOR 11
MARÍA JOSÉ ADROGUÉ 11

FOREWORD 13
GABRIEL SANCHEZ ZINNY 13
MARIANO NARODOWSKI 15
JORGE GOROSTIAGA 18

INTRODUCTION 23
1.1. PRESENTING THE PROBLEM 23
1.2. ACKNOWLEDGEMENT OF LIMITATIONS 26
1.3. CONCEPTUAL DELIMITATION 27
ON INCLUSION 28
ON INCLUSIVE EDUCATION 32
ON DISABILITY 34
1.4. QUESTIONS AND PURPOSE (BIOGRAPHY) 36

RESEARCH BACKGROUND: THE STATE OF THE ART 43

SURVEYS CONDUCTED BY CIVIL SOCIETY ORGANIZATIONS 53

THEORETICAL FRAMEWORK 57
4.1. EDUCABILITY, SCHOOL AND SCHOOL FAILURE 57
4.2. DISABILITY AND ITS DENOMINATIONS 61
4.3. SCHOOL MANAGEMENT, CHANGE AND LEADERSHIP 63
4.4. EDUCATION SYSTEM (AND SCHOOL CULTURE) 68
4.5. INSPECTORS AND SUPERVISORY SYSTEMS 72
4.6. THE SOCIOLOGICAL APPROACH TO SPECIAL EDUCATION, ACCORDING TO SALLY TOMLINSON 74
4.7 MEL AINSCOW AND TONY BOOTH´S INDEX FOR INCLUSION 79

DEVELOPMENT OF RESEARCH 83
5.1. THE EDUCATION SYSTEM OF THE PROVINCE OF BUENOS AIRES: ORGANIZATION 83
5.2. THE EDUCATION SYSTEM OF THE PROVINCE OF BUENOS AIRES: CHARACTERISTICS 89

- 5.3. METHODOLOGY: DESCRIPTIVE STUDY OF THE QUANTITATIVE TYPE 94
- 5.4. ADAPTING THE INDEX FOR INCLUSION TO THE STUDY: IMPLEMENTATION OF THE SURVEY THROUGH THE BODY OF INSPECTORS 101
- 5.5. PROCESSING OF DATA OBTAINED (TOOLS) 106

GENERAL RESULTS 109

- 6.1. PRELIMINARY QUESTIONNAIRE 109
  - PROFILE OF RESPONDENTS 109
  - RELATION WITH PEOPLE WITH DISABILITIES 114
- 6.2. GENERAL PERCEPTIONS OF INCLUSION 116
- 6.3. SURVEY QUESTIONNAIRE: VALUATION OF DIMENSIONS 119
  - 6.3.1. FIRST DIMENSION: CULTURES 119
  - 6.3.2. SECOND DIMENSION: POLICIES 124
  - 6.3.3. THIRD DIMENSION: PRACTICES 129
- 6.4. INTRA-DIMENSION CONSIDERATIONS 134
  - 6.4.1. EVOLVING INCLUSIVE CULTURES 134
  - 6.4.2. PRODUCING INCLUSIVE POLICIES 139
  - 6.4.3. DEVELOPMENT OF INCLUSIVE PRACTICES 144
- 6.5. ANALYSIS OF COMBINATIONS ACCORDING TO LEVEL, MODALITY AND LENGTH OF SERVICE OF EACH INSPECTOR 148

CONCLUSIONS AND POSSIBLE CONSIDERATIONS 157

CONCLUDING CONSIDERATIONS: A PROPOSAL FOR CHANGE 163

REFERENCES. 173

- 9.1 BOOKS, BOOK CHAPTERS, JOURNAL ARTICLES 173
- 9.2. DOCUMENTS, TREATIES, REPORTS AND LEGISLATION 181

ANNEX: QUESTIONNAIRE PROVIDED 185

- DATA COLLECTION FOR DIAGNOSIS 185
  - Status of Situation of Inclusion of Students with Disabilities in the Education system of the Province of Buenos Aires 185
- FIRST DIMENSION: CULTURES 187

ABOUT THE AUTHOR

María José Adrogué

Ms. Adrogué holds a law degree cum laude by the University of Buenos Aires, and holds a master's degree in education from the Torcuato Di Tella University. Founder of Educación Inclusiva ONG –Inclusive Education NGO– and of the Red Grupo Art. 24 por la Educación Inclusiva –Group Network Art. 24 for Inclusive Education–. Between 2017 and 2019 she served as Directora Provincial de Legal y Técnica de la Dirección General de Cultura y Educación de la Provincia de Buenos Aires –Head Legal Director of the Education Ministry of the Buenos Aires Province. She produced the documentary Oportunidades –Opportunities–, declared of social interest by the Legislature of the City of Buenos Aires and screened internationally (Geneva, New York) for the launch of the World Report on Disability by the WHO and the World Bank, 2011. She is married and has four children. She can speak Spanish, English, French and German.

FOREWORD

By Gabriel Sanchez Zinny, Mariano Narodoskwi and Jorge Gorostiaga

Gabriel Sanchez Zinny

How can we know if education systems are being inclusive? Furthermore, how can educational inclusion be defined? And why is so little research done on the inclusion of students with disabilities and the education policies that best promote it? How are these policies actually put into practice in schools?

The answers are eloquently argued by María José Adrogué in her recent book Education and Disability: Diagnosis and proposals for an inclusive school. In addition to reviewing the situation in the world, it includes comparative literature on the subject and the stance of different authors and organizations that fuel the debate on inclusion and on ways to expand it. But, unlike many educational books, it does not limit itself to diagnosis; the second part of this work focuses on a specific case, that of the Province of Buenos Aires, where Ms. Adrogué and myself worked together to carry out policies that expand opportunities for all students, particularly those with disabilities. Since the beginning of Governor Vidal's administration, the author has promoted these policies tirelessly, and has accurately executed many transformations that, despite the change of government, remain in force in the Province.

A clear example of this is the implementation of Resolution 1664/17 of the Federal Council of Education, aimed at strengthening, upholding and promoting the inclusion of students with disabilities in all kindergartens, primary and secondary schools. This regulation guarantees the freedom of choice of students and their families regarding what school to attend. At the same time, we modified the degree and certification system for students with disabilities. Students finishing secondary school will obtain a nationally valid certificate, which will enable them to continue their studies in any higher level institution.

Guaranteeing this certificate is recognizing that students with a disability have accessed contents with equal opportunities as the rest of their classmates, enhancing their possibilities and the development of their competences.

Apart from the importance of state policies, María José has understood -and expresses it throughout the book- the importance of civil society in promoting educational inclusion, in generating awareness throughout society, in exerting pressure not only on political, but also on business leaders. The author has promoted inclusion not only through this work, but also by founding several greatly influential civil organizations that are pioneers in the field in Argentina.

The research work also includes a very innovative survey on how the education system of the Province is perceived and the levels of inclusion of students, through questions to inspectors and school managers. As in other issues, the perception of inclusion is generally higher than the reality that is observed in many schools, but it maps out a path to be pursued and deepened, and to project the need for greater awareness and training.

We need to achieve a true paradigm shift in the conception of disability; as Adrogué says, "many current visions have at present stripped schools of their radical social importance: the experience of 'being capable of' that rejects the idea of a predetermined destiny, the school as that space where anyone can rise above themselves and that offers the world as a common good that belongs to everyone and that does not admit privileged owners".

Education and Disability is an essential book for all those involved and interested in improving education, in understanding the deep inequalities that exist in our country, particularly concerning a group of students receiving little attention and that are, still less, target of research. María José reflects upon and produces evidence on this, which generates a necessary debate and, hopefully, also the involvement of more sectors in this priority challenge in Argentina.

Gabriel Sánchez Zinny holds a Master's degree in Public Policy from Georgetown University; he is director of Blue Star Strategies (Washington DC) and is former Minister of Education of the Buenos Aires Province.

Mariano Narodowski

The issue of school inclusion is fertile ground for different and sometimes contradictory and overlapping discourses and proposals: since the mid-19th century, conceptualizations and theories have been outlined and developed about the working of a social system that allocates a valued public asset, education, and this task continues to be in the hands of specialists, pedagogues, policy makers and managers. Even at a time when the education system was being formed, it was clear a relationship was to be established between the personal experience of individuals and collective progress: a balance that few societies were able to strike satisfactorily.

While educational inclusion emerges as an implicit premise in the form of universality, despite the fact that, in the origins of education systems, access to school was a maximal aspiration, not a minimal one, the set of theoretical constructions produced back then continues to be an inspirational reference for many current theorists. Since the onset of the pansophical ideal of the 17th century and the revolutionary proclamations of 1789, everyone was to be educated (and that meant effectively everyone): the "General Enlightenment" project found in the so-called public regular school, the instrument -today we would say the technology- for its realization beyond the discursive proclamation.

Nowadays, the demands for more and better education for all are partly embodied in their potential beneficiaries, sometimes in their own voice, and sometimes in the different spokespersons and political and technical interpreters of these demands. This new scenario constitutes a second discursive nucleus around the idea of inclusion. It is now non-governmental institutions, such as social organizations, foundations, agencies, trade unions and other social groups and movements, which incorporate the concept of inclusion into their proclamations. These appear to be far removed from the state apparatus, statistical indices or doctrinaire objectives of the past, and closer to the life experience of those who are excluded, creating an aspiration for inclusion and, at times, an action plan and efforts to achieve it.

Finally, a third scenario emerges with notable impact: the fact that inclusion, by dint of its use as a slogan, becomes commonplace in proselytism and politically correct discourse. Thus, rendering the notion void of its original revolutionary and aspirational intent, and rather moving towards stereotypes ingrained in phrases, idioms and practices that pursue more than anything else an aesthetic objective, with little thoughtful and conscious concern for equalization or reparation.

For a long time now, the question has been posed as to how the important issues surrounding inclusion can be resolved. How can the question be formulated to facilitate understanding and affirmative action? How can effectively inclusive education policies be devised in a way that strips them of today's clichés?

This much-needed book by María José Adrogué is a lucid and rigorous attempt to provide potential answers to these questions under debate in political, technical and civil society circles, but which unfortunately have not led to an agenda for action.

The matter is not a simple one, given that one must first analyze and discuss the real educational experience of people, the organization of school availability and the specific diagnosis of the training processes of teachers and other professionals related to said people and organizations. Moreover, considering that all beneficiaries of the education system have special educational needs, this analysis needs to be wide-ranging and encompass the entire system.

This is why, despite the fact that the term inclusion has been widely used in connection with vulnerable populations and those whose rights have been denied, it is clear that only a comprehensive approach will lead to an accurate and effective response that levels the playing field to benefit those who have historically been excluded, the "stragglers" -those disparaged in a meritocratic race where the only ones bound to be successful, thanks to their relatively privileged starting point, will triumph.

Hence, María José Adrogué's views in this book summarize the need to consolidate the efforts of different sectors to provide education in accordance with the specific needs of each, based on a triad logic that compensates for inequalities, facilitating access, permanence and progress for those who need it most, and fosters both economic redistribution and cultural recognition.

In today's societies, including Argentina, teaching everything to everyone -the pansophical ideal that human knowledge is for all human beings- would be a mere euphemism if one fails to recognize societies' immense wealth of knowledge, and the fact that while the rate of the school-going population has grown enormously, it has done so in a brutally uneven manner, leading to increasingly growing pockets of socio-economic and cultural segregation compounded with exclusions of all kinds.

For this reason, the challenge of inclusion remains a current concern under new modes that are sensitive to more specific problems of vulnerable and (dis)abled sectors, in whom we identify deficiencies, not in terms of their respective ontic substance, but in the way they fit into a school organization historically designed for other supposedly non-deficient subjects.

If education is a public good of great relevance, and one in which we place many hopes and expectations, this poses an obligation to think about who the beneficiaries are and how these benefits are distributed. As Robert Connell argues, contrary to the democratizing proclamations of education systems, they tend to construct pyramid structure of sorts, where the number of people who access benefits narrows down as one reaches the vertex, with the pyramid growing narrower faster in poor countries, where the majority must be content if they receive a complete primary education, and whose marginalized sectors have enormous difficulties to integrate into the system due to the identification of certain deficiencies that impair them in light of the homogeneity of the offer.

In line with the reasoning behind María José Adrogué's study, the interests of the least favored should be prioritized, conceiving disability as a form of maladaptation of the school organization to individuals and not the other way round. In order for everyone to have access to a powerful and quality education regardless of their specific situation of birth or upbringing, it is necessary to combine these principles of redistribution, recognition and compensatory intervention.

Mariano Narodowski holds a PhD from the Universidade Estadual de Campinas (Brazil), is a full professor at the Universidad Torcuato Di Tella and former Minister of Education of the Autonomous City of Buenos Aires.

Jorge Gorostiaga

Over the last two decades, the education of people with disabilities as an area of study has gained visibility and traction in Argentina. This occurred simultaneously with the questioning -both in the academic realm and as part of educational practices- of the medical paradigm of disability, and its gradual replacement by the social paradigm. According to the latter, disability is not set within the body of the person with impairments, but rather in the environment that surrounds the person and which raises different types of obstacles to their full social insertion and participation. The change of perspective on this issue has posed the challenge of transforming the school experience in order to provide equal access to curricular and extracurricular activities. However, the significant regulatory advances achieved during the last few years contrast with persistent shortcomings in the design and implementation of policies -including the recording and publication of data- that would translate the principles and provisions of the regulations into effective execution in schools and higher educational institutions.

In our country's education system -as in most of the world- the situation of people with disabilities is part of a broader framework of relative (non-)fulfilment of the right to education and the reproduction of inequities, which particularly affects lower-income populations and various minorities. We live in an era in which the discourse of inclusion and expansion of rights have a strong legitimacy that cannot but be celebrated. However, as Sally Tomlinson (2015) -whose work is central to the development of the study reported in this book- as well as other referents of education sociology have remarked, schooling continues to act as a mechanism for perpetuating inequalities, categorizations and segregation. Insofar as the dynamics of inclusion/exclusion are inherent to contemporary education systems, understanding how they work -and continuing to investigate their specific manifestations in different contexts- is one of the keys to discussing policies and the form of school organization with a view to a future of justice and democratization.

The gradual adoption of the social model is clearly linked to reckoning access to education as a fundamental element towards the full social inclusion of people with disabilities. It is within this framework that the concept of inclusive education has been developed, as endorsed by the World Conference on Special Needs in Education (UNESCO, Salamanca, 1994). Initially associated with the education of people with disabilities, the concept has been broadened to include "equitable access to quality education without discrimination of any kind" (Blanco, 2014, Inclusión educative en américa Latina: caminos recorridos y por recorrer. In A. Marchesi, R. Blanco and A. Hernández (coordinators), Avances y desafíos de la educación inclusiva en Iberoamérica. Madrid: OEI). This is to be achieved through strategies that accept and value the diversity of learners, while focusing especially on those who have been excluded or who face greater risks of being marginalized based on their socio-economic background or minority status. At the global level, UNESCO has specifically insisted on promoting this broad-based approach, not restricted to learners with disabilities. Incorporating the notion of inclusive education (or, in other words, educational inclusion) has been an increasingly vital component of the reform agendas of international agencies, from the Education for All initiative (Jomtien Conference, 1990; Dakar Conference, 2000) to the more recent Education 2030 Framework for Action, derived from the Sustainable Development Goals established in 2015.

Beyond this broadened concept of inclusion, the analysis of debates and processes of policy design and material implementation of practices in education aimed at certain social groups remains an urgent task, and a certain necessity in the case of persons with disabilities.

In this sense, this book -derived from the author's master's thesis at the Torcuato Di Tella University- is an undoubtedly valuable contribution that places the issue in the Province of Buenos Aires and explores the views of key stakeholders, as are school inspectors. By way of synthesis and a schematic approach, María José Adrogué's work constitutes a contribution in at least three aspects:

It proposes and tests the adaptation of an Inclusion Index -originally designed to explore aspects of cultures, policies and practices of educational institutions- as applied to surveying perceptions about the degree of inclusiveness of an education system. The study, thus, sheds light on the use of an instrument that may be applicable to other stakeholders and education systems, and can be complemented with qualitative data creation/collection tools.

It performs a rigorous and thorough analysis of the empirical data obtained through the survey. Despite the constraints arising from data delimitation -in this case, determined mainly by the fact that the sample is not representative, and by the nature of the data collection instrument itself-, the study produces elements for diagnosis that, in turn, identifies potential areas of intervention to foster compliance with current regulations and spawn new actions for inclusion.

It presents a discussion of the results obtained and a proposal for change that adopts a clear position, contributing to the debate on controversial aspects worthy of consideration, such as the demand for greater participation of families in the schooling of learners with disabilities. Based on debatable but well-founded arguments, the author incites and questions all the stakeholders in the education system, in particular, as is logical, those most directly involved in working with students with disabilities under the special educational modality.

Throughout these pages, which convey the author's passion and commitment to the subject matter under analysis, certain tensions also arise within her own approach. Thus, for example, the celebration of diversity and the criticism of mechanisms of stigmatization or reproduction of inequalities is combined with ideas that are closer to the vision of a schooling system driven by the criteria of "usability", which -in the terms of Masschelein and Simons (2014), a reference used by Adrogué to discuss her results- detach said vision from its democratic and equalizing character. These tensions, far from invalidating arguments raised in the book or depriving them from consistency, reflect both the complexity and multiple sides to the phenomenon under analysis and the author's personal position.

In the current context of pandemic, the reading and discussion of this book is also pertinent for two reasons. On the one hand, the crisis situation unleashed by COVID-19 has dramatically highlighted the postponement of the demands and the violation of the rights of persons with disabilities, especially as regards to children and youths. On the other hand, it has raised new challenges for schools and education policies, which include redefining the role of families, and rethinking the strategies and instruments conducive to achieving the objectives of equality and the recognition of differences in the spheres and processes of access to knowledge.

Jorge Gorostiaga holds a PHD from Pittsburgh University (USA), is a full professor, researcher at CONICET and specialist in the analysis of education reforms in Latin America.

INTRODUCTION

1.1. PRESENTING THE PROBLEM

Nowadays, the word "inclusion" has extended its application to many areas of society, including educational and political realities. In the discussion on education policies, curriculum design, institutional management, pedagogy and other aspects related to education, the consideration of "inclusion" is an imperative issue on the agenda. Inclusion in general (social, economic), and educational inclusion in particular (possibly an unavoidable means to achieve the former), represents a true challenge in this new millennium (Romero, 2013), and constitutes a requisite for which -together with quality- we must take responsibility (Narodowski, 2018). It also embodies a challenge to education itself, from its very definition, as it imposes the need to redesign its selective social function to provide elements of social inclusion (Aguerrondo, 2008). The inclusion-exclusion binomial, as well as the concepts of equity and segregation, are now so integral to the education debate (Ball, 2013) that they have given rise to what is known as educational justice (see the interesting work of Veleda, Rivas and Mezzadra, 2011).

This general ethical imperative for greater inclusion (Amor Pan, 2007), coupled with the hard facts of reality (Fundación Par, 2006; Acuña, Goñi and Repetto, 2010; Echeita Sarrionandia, 2006a), and the reports of local civil society organizations before the UN Committee on the Rights of Persons with Disabilities (Edmund Rice International and Inclusive Education NGO, 2017; Grupo Artículo 24 por la Educación Inclusiva, 2017; Permanent Assembly for Human Rights et al., 2018) especially sparks our interest in delving into the issue in the country.

Our goal is to try to find out what is the current status of the largest education system in Argentina -in relation to inclusion-, which is also one of the main education systems in the American continent, in quantitative terms. We wish to do so not merely as a sample to gauge reality (in terms of the degree of inclusiveness of our schools), but rather as a starting point for the design of new inclusive education policies for the future, with an innovative and knowledgeable view of the school territory, based on the observations made by the body of inspectors, as a primary referent.

This is a fundamental question both from a political and pedagogical standpoint (Is it possible to educate everyone? How can we educate everyone in everything? Should we educate in a single or segregated manner?), and from a quantitative standpoint due to the size of the population and the number of educational establishments involved. The latest report by the World Bank and the World Health Organization, published in 2011, estimates that more than one billion people in the world live with some kind of disability -that is to say approximately 15 % of the world's population-, highlighting that around 785 million people (15.6 %) aged 15 and over have disabilities. The estimate at the time regarding the child population was 95 million children (5.1%), 13 million of whom (0.7%) suffer "severe disability", and this is a growing population. The World Health Organization summarizes the situation regarding disability with the following 10 hard facts:

> 1) More than 1 billion people have some form of disability; 2) disability disproportionately affects vulnerable populations; 3) people with disabilities often do not receive the health care they need; 4) children with disabilities are less likely to access the education system than children without disabilities; 5) people with disabilities are more likely to be unemployed than people without disabilities; 6) people with disabilities are vulnerable to poverty; 7) rehabilitation helps to maximize the ability to live a normal life and to strengthen independence; 8) people with disabilities can live and participate in the community; 9) disabling obstacles can be overcome; 10) the Convention on the Rights of Persons with Disabilities aims to promote, protect and ensure the enjoyment of human rights by all persons with disabilities. (World Health Organization, 2017).

In the particular case of Argentina, according to the 2014 National Population and Housing census, in one in five households there is a person with disability, and the prevalence is 12.9 % (Censo Nacional de Población, Hogares y Viviendas 2010, Serie C, 2014). However, recent studies for Argentina show some (downward) variations in prevalence rates, according to the pilot test carried out in the country in 2017, within the framework of the 2020 Census Round. Interpretations and definitions on disability, as well as the selection of certain age groups for sampling and their impact on the design of measurement instruments, have triggered efforts to establish general guidelines on the measurement of disability, such as those put forward by the Washington Group on Disability Statistics, within the framework of the United Nations Statistical Commission (see Argentine National Institute of Statistics and Censuses, 2019).

This data is set against legislation at global, national and provincial levels that encourages the inclusion of people with disabilities. However, while regulations advocate the inclusion of children with disabilities in schools, its effective implementation is scarce (Mendía at Fundación Par, 2005; Echeita Sarrionandia, 2006a; Acuña, Goñi and Repetto, 2010; Blanco Guijarro, 2006). The latest reports submitted in 2017 by civil society organizations to the United Nations regarding compliance with the International Convention on the Rights of Persons with Disabilities in Argentina, specifically concerning their right to inclusive education, are a testament to the foregoing statement. In addition to the scarce implementation of inclusion policies, there is a general lack of interest in the quality of special education in Argentina, which for various reasons is overlooked by standardized evaluations, both at national and international level (PISA, Aprender), despite an initial innovative experience carried out in the Province of Buenos Aires in 2019[1] . This scenario spurred the decision to probe into the situation of the education system of the Province of Buenos Aires with regard to the inclusion of students with disabilities. To do so, we based our

---

1   Said "Province of Buenos Aires Evaluation of Learning in Special Education", conducted by the General Directorate of Culture and Education, was performed in 20 schools, located in 13 districts, corresponding to 8 educational regions, involving the participation of 152 students, 48 teacher agents, and 20 observers, the objective of which was to account for the knowledge and skills developed in the areas of Language Practices and Mathematics (Dirección General de Cultura y Educación de la Provincia de Buenos Aires, 2019).

analysis on the perception of the members of the supervisory team of the Province of Buenos Aires, given that they are responsible for inspecting schools on aspects as broad as their functioning, structure, practices and compliance with policies, among other issues.

At the same time, we aimed to identify the dimensions of the school reality that are most compromised: policies, cultures or practices.

1.2. ACKNOWLEDGEMENT OF LIMITATIONS

Prudence dictates that we begin by acknowledging certain limitations or weaknesses. Readers will surely find more of them, but the following are those that, a priori, we have identified and assume. Thus, this research:

- Does not intend to, nor can it be considered an all-inclusive survey of the education system of the Province of Buenos Aires.

- Does not seek to characterize the institutions of said education jurisdiction from the perspective of school micro-politics or school organization theory (Ball, 2012), nor does it intend to impose the theory of Sociology of Special Education (Tomlinson 2012, 2014) as the only explanation for the development of this modality.

- Only proposes adopting a macro level -that of an education system- for those school dimensions identified by Ainscow and Booth (2002) to measure the level of inclusion perceived regarding their schools.

- The measurement and assessment of each of the components that make up these dimensions was performed by the inspection or supervision team of the Province of Buenos Aires, that is to say, the surveys were answered by members of the General Inspection Office of the Directorate-General for Culture and Education of Buenos Aires.

- The latter probably entails some degree of bias, since the same people responsible for the management of the education system (which claims to be inclusive) are the ones who weigh the proposed items. For this reason, in addition to applying the rating for levels of inclusion ranging from very inclusive, to relatively inclusive, to not very inclusive (Inclusion Index), we made a point of reviewing the potential relationship between the survey answers provided and the preliminary questionnaire given to each inspector (referring to personal and/or professional characteristics), to detect possible patterns. For said search, the sociological approach proposed by Tomlinson (2012, 2014) was particularly useful.

- The inspirational use of the Inclusion Index, designed for educational institutions, and its subsequent adaptation to create an index that encompasses an entire education system is a challenge in itself. This task was undertaken in the belief that, despite the limitations of the approach, it can yield results that contribute to identifying the areas that demand most urgent work on the inclusion of students with disabilities. We hope that this assessment -particularly in terms of which dimension (cultures, policies or practices) is perceived as having a higher or lower level of inclusion- will constitute a useful input for the development of programs and implementation plans for greater inclusion in schools.

1.3. CONCEPTUAL DELIMITATION

Lastly, this introduction requires pointing out three conceptual concerns because the meanings of the underlying concepts permeate the entire content of the work: (i) what do we refer to when we talk about inclusion; (ii) what do we understand by disability; and (iii) what is considered inclusive education.

These are three malleable concepts whose meanings and limits are sensitive to worldviews and ideologies, as well as the passing of time and changes in reality, which is why it is imperative to try to define them, at least in terms of their intended meaning within this work. There is no intention to postulate the correctness or incorrectness of any particular meaning or to disqualify other possible meanings, but rather to clarify the issue with intellectual honesty for the better delimitation of this study and understanding of the statements in it. However, the acknowledgement of different notions of inclusive education does not imply the adoption of a relativistic position that assigns identical value to all conceptions. Under Booth and Ainscow, we understand that each perspective constitutes a view connected to a system of values, and expresses a commitment in some particular direction for the development of practices that necessarily implies some degree of criticism of the other positions. The debate is enriched and becomes more honest when authors make their views explicit, as this somehow leads them to explore said views critically and avoid their own inconsistencies (Booth and Ainscow, 1998).

ON INCLUSION

The word inclusion usually refers to a set of groups or "collectives", mainly minority groups defined by race, religion, nationality, sex, disability, etc. The value of inclusion, development and the possibility of empowering each individual and their community are presented as undisputed, non-negotiable aspirations recognized throughout the world, especially since the 1990 Jomtien Conference on Education for All, followed by the 1994 Salamanca World Conference (UNESCO).

"Inclusion is inclusion": the word in itself implies non-exclusion, and therefore, it shall mean the inclusion of all without excluding anyone, thus it would seem an oxymoron to raise the issue of inclusion with respect to a specific population group (in this case, students with disabilities). The phenomenon of school exclusion -and its remedy, inclusion- is also raised by Tomlinson (2012; 2014), and Ainscow and Booth (2002a, 2002b) in broad terms and with the greatest amplitude. In this sense, the inclusive school is that which receives, takes into consideration for the design of teaching and learning strategies, and values all students in the community, without limiting said inclusion to the case of students with disabilities. Their aspiration -and the author´s- is that the same school and educational service for all provide an education with a broader and more comprehensive view, in which the school responds to the diversity of all students regardless of their categorization into groups with special needs or disability (Booth and Ainscow, 1998). Thus, inclusive education would not be limited to the comprehensive school movement, nor to the complaisant treatment of students with disabilities, those that misbehave, or belong to vulnerable groups. Inclusion actually refers to a dynamic process of increasing elimination of obstacles for learning and participation. This, in a way, implies an aspiration or a movement towards an ideal (that of full inclusion in one and the same education for all, without the need for special, integrated, adapted, or even inclusive education). Notwithstanding, this does not necessarily render it an unattainable illusion or a chimera (as the illusion of a single perspective on the matter would appear to be), but rather an ongoing process.

In spite of the foregoing, the organization of the education system in Argentina differentiates a particular group (that of students with disabilities) as the recipient of a different kind of educational service; there is only one modality directly and expressly linked to the individual characteristics of the student: Special Education. Although there are other modalities linked to groups that make up minorities (e.g., education in the context of confinement, hospital education), these take into consideration the current circumstances surrounding the student at the given moment (deprivation of liberty, inability to attend school premises), but without reference to their individual characteristics and/ or abilities. Even the provision of the modality for ethnic minorities (intercultural bilingual education) is more a recognition of a collective right (as it refers to indigenous peoples and not to individuals or students) than of an individual one.

Let's see: National Education Law 26206, in its Title II "The Education System" provides for the organization of 12 education levels and/ or modalities: pre-school, primary, secondary, higher, technical-professional, artistic, special, permanent for youths and adults, rural, intercultural bilingual, in contexts of confinement, and home/hospital. The pre-school and primary school levels correlate with students in accordance to their ages, and the following cycles (secondary and higher) are conceived mainly as instances for the continuity of education, aimed at those who have completed the previous levels. Once these education levels have been established, modalities are defined which take into account different issues, namely: (a) specific vocational orientations (technical-professional and artistic); (b) circumstances specific to the environment or the life of individuals in terms of their possibility to access educational institutions (education in rural areas, in the context of deprivation of liberty, and home and hospital education); or (c) characteristics of its students, be it in terms of their age (permanent education for youths and adults), their origin (intercultural bilingual education), or their individual characteristics (special education for people with disabilities). It would seem that the system proposes, from the normative point of view, that the special educational modality be provided in the same regular educational institutions in accordance to the education levels, and not in segregated areas[2] . The Province of Buenos Aires, on the other hand, organizes its education system in Law 13688, Chapter II, observing the levels of education and modalities set forth by the national legislation, but providing for additional modalities (physical education, community psychology and social, environmental, intercultural pedagogy), while also providing for a new classification of the educational service according to the setting in which it is developed (Chapter XV, Sections 46 to 54): urban, rural continental and island environments, confinement, home and hospital contexts, as well as virtual environments. In the normative organization of the education system of the Province of Buenos Aires, thus, the point made above regarding the national legislation is even clearer, in that special education is the only modality foreseen for a minority of the population defined by its particular characteristics, especially given that the intercultural educational modality is articulated with all levels, and not addressed to a specific group of people, but rather to all students in the education system, as do the other new modalities (physical, psychological, etc.). Hospital or home-based education (which are usually associated with special education) is defined in relation to its context of execution, as noted above.[3]

---

[2] Section 42 of the National Education Law 26206 establishes that: "Special Education is the education system modality aimed at ensuring the right to education for people with disabilities, be they temporary or permanent, at all levels and modalities of the Education System. Special Education is governed by the principle of educational inclusion, in accordance with Section 11, Subsection n) of this Law. Special Education provides educational attention for all those specific issues that cannot be addressed by regular education. The Ministry of Education, Science and Technology, in agreement with the Federal Council of Education, shall guarantee the integration of students with disabilities in all levels and modalities according to the possibilities of each individual."

[3] Law 13688, Section 39, provides the following definition of special education: "Special Education is the modality responsible for guaranteeing the integration of students with disabilities, be they temporary or permanent, at all Levels according to the possibilities of each individual, assuring them the right to education, as well as providing them with educational attention in all those specific issues that cannot be addressed exclusively by common education, and facilitating complementary pedagogical proposals. Special Education is governed by the principle of educational inclusion, in accordance with the provisions of this Law, for which it allocates educational resources to participate in the education of children as from the very moment of birth. The Directorate-General for Culture and Education shall guarantee the integration of students with temporary or permanent disabilities at all levels according to the possibilities of each individual

Despite the fact that the definition of the special educational modality in the legislation of the Province of Buenos Aires (Law 13688, Section 39) includes the principle of educational inclusion, it cannot be clearly stated -as is set forth in the national legislation- that said modality is to be provided in the same regular educational institutions in accordance with the education levels, and not in segregated environments. This is due to the fact that, while the subsequent section (Law 13688, Section 40, Subsection f) refers to "the physical accessibility of all school buildings" when establishing the procedures and resources of the Directorate-General for Culture and Education to ensure the right to education and school integration, there is a previous reference to "the coverage of special educational institutions" (Subsection d).

In any case, this disengagement between the premise for greater educational inclusion and the special educational modality reflected in legislation still seem far in the future. It is a sign of the contradiction and the amalgamation that current circumstances imprint on education systems, which, at the same time as they become increasingly competitive and receive a greater number of students (many of whom are children who do not perform according to the required standards), they require greater support services in mainstream schools. Namely, special education in regular schools, aimed at that growing number of children identified as having "special educational needs" and whose parents demand inclusion (in regular schools) and specialized attention (special education) (Tomlinson, 2014). The existence of a specific educational modality for the population minority defined by its particular characteristics -people with disabilities- and, on this basis, selected as a differentiated recipient of educational services in the largest educational district of our country, warrants that we heighten our efforts to review the concept of inclusion of students with disabilities. The delimitation of the term inclusion for the purposes of this study does not imply denying that the origin of this segregation of children with disabilities (which operates as a necessary condition for subsequent inclusion) may be shared, in sociological terms, with the identification of other disadvantaged minorities -coexisting with normative and non-normative categories and the debate on social selection- to finally give way to the premise (considered less stigmatizing but much more encompassing) of "special needs" (Tomlinson, 2012), under whose umbrella usually lies an attempt to remedy the exclusion of these other excluded groups. In this study, therefore, focus will be placed on the inclusion of students with disabilities (including the blended notion that admits the combination of the medical model and the social model, as will be explained below).

ON INCLUSIVE EDUCATION

As for the concept of Inclusive Education, in the present study, its meaning applies to the particular case of children with disabilities and their admittance to regular schools (that is to say, mainstream education). We are aware that this approach of considering Inclusive Education only that in which the student with a disability is admitted to regular schools (and not to special education schools) gives rise to opposition. There are those who argue that inclusive education is achieved when students with disability are admitted to the "education system", whereas belonging to the special modality would be a way to accomplish their education, in terms of inclusion. This study adopts the opposite position, not only because of the theoretical framework used as a point of reference ("inclusive education consists in the increasing participation of all students in their neighborhood, in their school of residence", Booth and Ainscow, 1998: 3), but also in light of an alignment with international documents (Salamanca Declaration, UNESCO, 1994), and the guidelines for the interpretation of supranational regulations (International Convention on the Rights of Persons with Disabilities, UN, 2006) established by international organizations, which consider it a segregating and discriminatory practice for the educational service of children with disabilities to be provided in schools organized to cater exclusively for students with disabilities. This was pointed out by the Office of the United Nations High Commissioner for Human Rights in its Thematic Study.[4]

The justification for this quotation (which implies the admission of an international stakeholder as an interpretative source of the regulations)

---

4 It explains: "Segregation occurs when a student with said characteristics is referred to an educational institution specifically designed to respond to a particular impairment, usually in a special education system. (...) The inclusive education approach has emerged in response to these discriminatory approaches. As stated in its preface, the Salamanca Statement and Framework for Action on Special Needs Education is inspired by the recognition of the need to act towards 'schools for all' - that is, institutions that include everyone, celebrate differences, support learning and respond to everyone's needs" (UN, A/HRC/25/29, 2013, par. 4 and 5).

becomes unquestionable if the phenomenon of globalization and the transnational regulation of education systems is accepted. Although this study deliberately omits a legal analysis and an account of related regulations, simply reading this introductory chapter reveals a network of regulations of different nature (origin and scope) that outline inclusive education: communiques, provisions, resolutions of a bureaucratic-administrative nature (in this case, originating in the Directorate-General for Culture and Education of the Province of Buenos Aires), laws issued by both the provincial legislature and the National Congress, resolutions issued by the Federal Council of Education, provincial and national constitutions, as well as international treaties and conventions (to which Argentina adheres) which are incorporated into the legal system with supra-constitutional rank. In this regard, bearing in mind that the movement for the inclusion of people with disabilities originated at an international level, the work of Gorostiaga (2020) is particularly relevant. Based on the theory of the regulation of education systems and the diversity of its sources, his work clearly displays the phenomenon of transnational regulation of education systems (from a political standpoint). He portrays a scenario in which there are many stakeholders (public authorities, coalitions of organizations, professional associations) and where global reform movements are led by multilateral entities, not only in terms of proposals, but also in terms of post-bureaucratic regulation, through the publication of reports with different approaches (humanistic, economistic or rights-based, depending on the entity in question) which legitimize certain educational problematizations, and thus drive education reforms.

Coming back to the delimitation of the object of study herein addressed, notwithstanding the foregoing, it is worth noting that this analysis will focus on inclusion in the education system of the Province of Buenos Aires as a whole -that is to say, including in the assessment its special schools and the participation of the inspectors of this modality in the sample. Thus, the adoption of a particular standpoint on the definition of Inclusive Education (and whether it is achieved in regular schools or in special schools) should be admitted as an element of criticism of the results obtained. If the instrument inspired by the Index for Inclusion developed by Ainscow and Booth is applied to the sample taken, the aforementioned standpoint is disregarded, and the inclusion score will refer to the system in general, irrespective of the educational modalities.

ON DISABILITY

Let us now turn to the concept of disability, given that just like what is known as "inclusive education", it has also been the subject of important changes. The idea behind disability has changed over time. On the one hand, the currents that postulated the medical model of disability place exclusive emphasis on the biological impairment of the person. On the other hand, the social model of disability qualifies the social environment as "disabling", attributing all responsibility to the social and physical obstacles that stymie the adequate performance of people (Maldonado, 2013). While both positions have been presented as dichotomous, it is now accepted that disability must be approached from a mixed or eclectic perspective that recognizes the different nuances of this complex phenomenon: disability is a result of the dynamic interaction between health conditions and contextual factors, both personal and environmental (World Health Organization and World Bank, 2011). This is, thus, the key to reflect on the role of the school institution in general (is it a disabling environment or an enabling space?), considering each school in particular, and the education system they make up, in the face of a population of students frequently labeled as having "special educational needs", who reclaim to be included in school life. The very notion of disability -its origin, development, and variations- constitutes an extremely interesting and complex issue; although the idea of disability is a primary constituent of the concept of Inclusive Education, its particular approach deserves a study in itself (Buitrago Echeverri and Lara Bernal, 2013; Torres González, 2010). Just as the concept of disability has undergone important changes, so has the education of people with disabilities. At first, people with disabilities were rejected by the education system in general, then admitted, yet segregated from the regular system, to be currently welcome under progressively more inclusive modalities (Echeita Sarrionandia, 2006b; Vivar, Delgado, Corona and García, 2011; Verdugo Alonso, 2003; Moya Maya, Martínez Ferrer and Ruiz Salguero, 2012; Grañeras, Lamelas, Segalerva, Vázquez, Gordo and Molinuevo, 1998; González García, 2009). Segregation, integration and inclusion constitute evolving stages (Blanco Guijarro, 2006; Opertti and Belalcázar, 2008) within the phenomenon of school universalization. The concept of inclusive education has developed in step with the actual changes in the schooling of children with disabilities. However, despite the normative and practical advances both worldwide and at national level in Argentina, and even locally in the Province of Buenos Aires, school inclusion of children with disabilities is far from being a consolidated reality. The education of this population group presents a reality with obstacles in their admittance, acreditación (contents learnt), promotion, graduation and certificación (level passed) in regular schools. There is an ample variety of scenarios, especially in the case of privately managed institutions, where school autonomy is heightened: total inclusion in all areas, integration depending on whether curricular or extracurricular subjects are involved, shared classrooms, differentiated spaces, handling of different disabilities or specialization in one type of disability, to name just a few aspects.

Admittedly, each experience may present certain advantages (or disadvantages), but it is understood that equity and educational justice proposed by different specialties or approaches, such as the management of social change (Bang and Vossoughi, 2016), its advantages in economic-social development (Levin, 2008), educational inclusion as a means for social justice (Polat, 2011) or as a matter of ethics (Amor Pan, 2007), and as recognition of the ultimate moral purpose of education -to enable change in the lives of the students to empower them as active citizens in increasingly complex societies- (Fullan, 1993) impose the need to build a basis for inclusion in each and every one of the institutions that make up the education system, and for all its students, so that everyone can develop their potential and have the tools for self-empowerment inherent to adult life, in the school closest to their home, within their community. One can only start to think about the construction of quality inclusion on the basis of real data: it is necessary to know how inclusive the country's largest education system is -or is perceived to be-.

1.4. QUESTIONS AND PURPOSE (BIOGRAPHY)

The question posed in this study refers to the level of inclusion and the different dimensions that this system presents. Specifically, the query is: How inclusive is the education system of the Province of Buenos Aires, according to the perception of the agents of the School Inspection Office, as per the parameters and dimensions of the "Index for Inclusion" by Tony Booth and Mel Ainscow? Derived from this main question, and from the application of a survey that proposes three general variables corresponding to the three dimensions of analysis pertaining to the reality of school inclusion (creation of inclusive cultures, formulation of inclusive policies and development of inclusive practices), the following questions ensue: What is the general level of inclusion of the education system in the Province of Buenos Aires, as per the proposed dimensions? Is the system considered very inclusive, somewhat inclusive or not very inclusive? Are there differences between the general ratings and the ratings for each dimension? Are any dimensions rated as more inclusive than others? On a different note, with respect to the position (role, hierarchy, seniority, etc.) of the inspector in the system, the question posed is whether it is possible to establish any relationship between teacher training and/or performance field (special modality, state or private school, school inspector or regional inspector, etc.), or personal characteristics (sex, length of service, age) and the perception of the level of inclusion.

With the foregoing, needless to say, the general objective of the present work is to offer elements for diagnosis -based on the perception derived from inspection- of the level of inclusion of the education system of the Province of Buenos Aires, according to the categories and dimensions proposed by Ainscow and Booth.

The goal is, thus, to identify the perceived level of inclusion for each one of the dimensions (cultures, policies and practices) of the education system in the Province of Buenos Aires, so as to draw an inclusion perception score for each dimension and for the education system as a whole. Additionally, the aim is to analyze the correlation between the perception of inclusion and the respondents' own data (training, level or modality, length of service, etc.) in accordance with the Sociology of Special Education developed by Sally Tomlinson. Finally, the study seeks to explore the use of the Inclusion Index as a guideline for the education system diagnostic tool to be employed and its usefulness in triggering educational change towards the implementation of initiatives for greater inclusion.

Notwithstanding the fact that this is a quantitative, descriptive study, the characteristics of the object of study (pertaining to the social sciences) and the purpose of the research (to build greater educational inclusion in the Province of Buenos Aires) would render the foregoing clarifications, limitations and conceptual delimitation incomplete unless they include an explanation of the philosophical paradigm adopted and a personal reference regarding the choice of, and interest in, the chosen subject matter. To do so, reference will be made to John Creswell (2013), who, despite referring especially to qualitative research, presents some classifications of approaches and suggestions that are also relevant here.

Thus, with regard to our conceptual framework, philosophical assumptions or interpretative framework, the classification proposed by the aforementioned author, between those interpretative frames of reference derived from theories of social sciences and those of social justice, is very useful.

The first group includes paradigms related with positivism, realism, social constructivism, interpretivism and hermeneutics, transformational approaches, postmodern perspectives, pragmatism, feminist theories, critical race theory, the queer paradigm and the disability paradigm. The preceding list is merely illustrative, as perspectives are constantly expanding. Moreover, a combination of theories or perspectives may be used for conducting the analysis and research. In this case, the starting point is a realist position in ontological terms, in the sense the study is based on the understanding that the world exists independently of our beliefs or theoretical constructions, despite being compatible with constructivist epistemology (Becerra, 2018), which concludes that knowledge is a construction of its own, mainly due to our pragmatic perspective. The purpose of this research is to contribute to the transformation of the educational reality. To do so, one must understand the view of the main stakeholders in the system, distinguish small subsystems or categories, for which a theoretical framework is selected in the belief that it is suitable for achieving the goal, irrespective of whether or not to its underlying premise is adhered to. Such is the case of the theory of the Sociology of Special Education, rooted in the critical race theory, and even the paradigm of disability, which postulates a sociological concept of disability.[5]

In the case under analysis, the referred pragmatism justifies the reference to a wide and varied selection of authors that help identify the main pieces that make up the puzzle that is the reality of school inclusion. This includes the concept of school and its role, universal educability and the phenomenon of school failure, the concept of disability, the view on school management, the change and leadership required by innovations, the characterization of education systems, their dynamics and school culture.

Though these frameworks of concepts and outlooks make up the general issue, for the purpose of assessing school inclusion in the education system of the Province of Buenos Aires and its "measurement" (according to the opinions of the provincial supervision team members) a special theoretical framework is adopted, based on the dimensions used by Ainscow and Booth to create the Index for Inclusion, and the positions, biases and interests proposed by Sally Tomlinson's Sociology of Special Education. These approaches are particularly useful for the understanding of the phenomenon, and thus enable the detection of focal points (dimensions) and positions on which new inclusion plans and programs should (or could) be designed.

Having said this, continuing in line with Creswell (2013), a personal reference is due regarding the choice of topic, and background information about myself, as author of this study. I come from a family of professionals (medical doctors and lawyers) characterized by a strong belief in the decisive power of education for the vital development of all people. Moreover, our religious upbringing forged a definite commitment to become personally involved in changing reality (we

---

[5] The allusion in this paper to the Sociology of Special Education as the main theoretical framework (and, in particular, to the theory developed by Sally Tomlinson) does not imply that it is the only sociological approach to this subject. The same clarification should be made with respect to the paradigm of disability, an issue on which different theories and approaches coexist.

would say, contributing to "building the Kingdom"), all of which, together with my undergraduate education as a lawyer, led to a strong vocation towards preventing situations of injustice and violation of rights -especially when they impact on the possibilities of personal development and progress- of those who are most vulnerable. Within this context and upbringing environment, a child with intellectual disabilities was born to our inner-family nucleus. After reflection on the child's education, the search for a vacancy in a regular school became an odyssey that, although successfully resolved in the particular case, made a hitherto unknown reality flagrantly evident: hundreds of families without resources or training, whose children or grandchildren were systematically rejected from mainstream education, and were finally left out of the general education system due to the family difficulties involved in schooling in a special school (which is generally far from home, and is not the one that other members of the family group may attend, not to mention the high cost of tuition in the case of privately run schools). It was, thus, an ethical imperative -with decisive influence of the work of Amor Pan as part of our education- that fueled my interest in the issue of inclusion of people with disabilities, together with the strong belief there is an urgent and vital need to provide education to those who need it most: a deprivation of rights that should appall any well-trained lawyer.

After talking to school managers, teachers and families, we decided that the priority was to raise awareness among educational institutions and managers, so we created and produced a documentary film called "Oportunidades" (Adrogué M.J. and Septiembre Films, 2010) which had the support of international organizations such as the World Health Organization, Unicef and the Order of Malta, and was presented at the opening of the UN inauguration ceremony of the World Report on Disability in the cities of Geneva and New York (2011). The documentary was declared of social interest by the Legislature of the City of Buenos Aires, and presented in educational institutions by the Ministry of Education of the City of Buenos Aires, during the Special Education Week (2011). This prompted the foundation of EDUCACIÓN INCLUSIVA ONG, with the mission of providing consultancy in educational inclusion, establishing institutional alliances (among them, the national network "Grupo Art. 24 por la Educación Inclusiva"), and contributing to the visibility and awareness regarding the educational situation of people with disabilities to have an impact on public policies (including a report on the status of compliance with the Convention on the Rights of Persons with Disabilities before the UN Monitoring Committee in 2017).

My personal interest and professional need to acquire deeper knowledge and understanding of the teaching world led me once again to become engaged in the university environment and to public office, as Director of Legal and Technical Affairs of the Directorate-General for Culture and Education of the Province of Buenos Aires, the highest position of legal responsibility concerning the educational portfolio of the Province of Buenos Aires. This position provided a macro-level perspective of the functioning and organization of the education system, and allowed me to visit regular and special education schools on a weekly basis, share our work with the Supervision Directorate as well as with the Directorates of Level and Modality, and, especially, work on the enactment of local regulations that would decisively and clearly advance towards greater inclusion of students with disabilities.

However, considering that the inclusion of students with disabilities is a multidimensional phenomenon and a process in permanent development, it seemed imperative that we should know more about the level of inclusion within each dimension, so that the revision of practices, cultures and policies, pursuant to the diagnosis of those in charge of the inspection of all schools in the Province, may constitute a valuable input to reinforce educational change that advances efforts towards a greater degree of effective inclusion. Lastly, though it may seem unnecessary, it should be highlighted that the circumstance of my being in the public office while the survey was conducted did not produce methodological or interpretative interferences or biases: in order to ensure this, I made it a point of stressing the greatest possible adherence to the original Index used as a guideline, and subjected the results to peer review by another member of the technical staff. In addition, the survey was conducted during a general meeting (without prior preparation of the inspectors, to ensure the spontaneity of responses), and the data processing and analysis was carried out once I had left public office. Finally, it is worth noting that the results of the survey were completely unrelated to my own responsibilities, that is, to my political-professional area of competence, so there was no interest at any time in showing certain levels of inclusion, but rather to unveil -to the extent possible- the perception of this phenomenon and its different aspects.

2

RESEARCH BACKGROUND: THE STATE OF THE ART

There is probably no better way to form a fairly complete picture of any issue to be studied than to review the relevant publications, and thus detect not only similar studies, but also different approaches to reality, and even new elements surrounding it. It is therefore appropriate to review them here.

As said when presenting the problem, educational inclusion is currently the subject of study of countless publications. Some works address educational inclusion from the perspective of management and leadership (Murillo, Krichesky, Castro and Hernández, 2010), to the extent of proposing a new type of leadership called "inclusive" (Romero, 2013). Although they usually refer to inclusion not in terms of students with disabilities, but rather in terms of students belonging to culturally, socially and economically disadvantaged groups or populations, it could well be extrapolated to the case of disability inclusion.

On the other hand, there are several works on teaching or learning methods for children with disabilities or special educational needs (Valdez, 2012), and even on the technological tools available to enable meaningful learning (Maldonado, 2020). These publications tend to focus on the psychological aspects or limitations of each pathology or condition - e.g., deaf students, students with Down syndrome, intellectual disabilities, TGD or autism spectrum, Asperger's, sensory limitations, etc. - for their adequate pedagogical approach (Benavides, 2007), rather than focusing on school management as a project in itself or, consequently, on the characteristics of the school's institutional management. Even less so, on the education system of which it is a part. In the aforementioned line of schooling "guidelines", the contributions and systematizations presented in the works of Levine (2003) and Bonals and Sánchez-Cano (2007), and the survey of technological tools by Maldonado (2020) are particularly valuable.

From a different perspective, important works of data collection and systematization, censuses and information surveys attempt to give an account of the real situation of the population with disabilities: research that confronts the premises of inclusive education with the daily reality of its effective attainment. In the local context of Argentina, the works of Acuña, Goñi and Repetto (2010) and Fundación Par (2005) are particularly relevant, as they make it possible to evaluate the relationship between general regulations and institutional policy. From a global perspective, the works of Artiles, Kozleski and Waitoller (2011), Ainscow (2007) and Echeita Sarrionandia (2006b), among others, should be taken into consideration.

The selection and coordination of research presented -and commented on, and even criticized- by Booth and Ainscow (1998) is particularly relevant. In their work "From them to us", different authors conduct research on the experiences of student inclusion in educational institutions in different parts of the world. In particular, the cases of the United States of America, Scotland, New Zealand, Norway, the Netherlands, Ireland, Australia and England are frequent subjects of study. Although each study in said book focuses on inclusion practices implemented in one or two schools, and in relation to a single student or a small group of students with disabilities or belonging to a minority or disadvantaged sector, each author contrasts, to some degree, the characteristics of the type of school inclusion implemented by the school under analysis pursuant to the regulatory or bureaucratic organization of the education system in which it is immersed, but they fail to draw conclusions on the manner and the extent to which these education systems are inclusive in general terms. Another particularity of this compilation work is that it highlights (especially in the articles by its coordinators) the different notions of inclusion and the inconsistencies likely to be encountered when this subject matter is studied if there is no awareness of the fact that educational inclusion must be understood in relation to the unconditional inadmissibility of any and all forms of exclusion. Hence, the initial statement of the position adopted herein.

The referred work of selection, guidance and compilation led by Booth and Ainscow predates the development of the Inclusion Index, and one might venture to think that, perhaps, it was the variety (and even the contradiction) of views on and assessments of the level of inclusion of the schools reported therein, whether their practices could be considered segregating, or proper (and appropriate) of an adapted education (special education in the regular school or mainstream education), which may raise the alert on the need to create an index with common and objective parameters, observable by the members of the school community themselves, that would make it possible to measure the level of inclusion of each school regardless of which practice is considered inclusive by each evaluator, teacher or researcher. Only on the basis of constructing consensus around concrete and observable practices, could the process of change (cultural, normative, etc.) take place in the educational institution and radiate into the entire system.

Finally, one cannot overlook publications that focus on the criticism of the school institution insofar as its grammar, its devices and its "normalizing" approach to the student are deemed contrary to the fundamental respect for singularities, a necessary condition for the development of the many, few or varied potentialities of each student (Lus, 1995; Baquero, 2002; Baquero and Narodowski, 1991; Skliar, 2005; Sosa, 2005; Sosa, 2005; Skliar, 2005; Sosa, 2008; Vain 2005, 2006), as well as other research that highlights the characteristics of the Special Educational modality, its strengths and weaknesses, and analyzes the tensions between special and inclusive education (Fuchs and Fuchs, 1993; Andrews, Carnine, Coutinho, Edgar, Forness, Fuchs, Jordan, Kauffman, Patton, Rosell, Rueda, Schiller, Skrtic, & Wong, 2000; Ferri, Gallagher, & Connor, 2011), and thus propose new school strategies to address the teaching of students with difficulties and/or disabilities (Fuchs & Fuchs, 1994; 1998; 2009; Fuchs, Fuchs, & Bishop, 1992; Rueda, 2011; Klingner and Boardman, 2011).

However, and despite the connection between the aforementioned studies and central aspects of the present research, none of them proposes an attempt to measure the level of (perceived) inclusion with respect to an education system, based on Ainscow and Booth's Index for Inclusion, and then shed light on the results obtained through the lens of Sally Tomlinson's Sociology of Education. Some studies do engage in the adaptation and/or application of the Index for Inclusion not just to a particular school but to a group of schools and/or larger communities and other contexts, and even wonder about its validity or possibilities of application with respect to other education systems different from the one for which it was designed. Some works can be found along these lines, though none of them for Argentina.

Castro Rubilar, Castañeda Díaz, Ossa-Cornejo, Blanco-Hadi and Castillo-Valenzuela (2017) propose, based on the adaptation of the Ainscow and Booth Index for Inclusion, a new measurement instrument on the acceptance and predisposition for school inclusion called "Inclusive Self-Ascription Scale", the purpose of which is to establish an individual (personal) measurement criterion by teachers and managers, based on beliefs and attitudes of inclusion acceptance. This scale was implemented by way of interviews with 548 teachers from a representative sample of secondary schools in the town of Ñuble, Chile. While the results highlight certain specific elements, they are still grouped under the three dimensions proposed by the Index for Inclusion. The research starts off from the problem of the absence of an instrument in Spanish on the readiness for inclusion, especially in the case of an education system characterized -both at the policy and management levels- by a strong bureaucratic-curricular profile in decision-making, which is an obstacle for the processes of diversity and inclusion of students.

The work of Deppeler and Harvey (2004) begins by reviewing the validation (and modification) of the Index for Inclusion in a six-phase process, and then applies it to assess the efficacy and sustainability of a comprehensive school approach and its impact on improving inclusive practices, strengthening networks (outside the school) and improving the learning of students with disabilities in Catholic primary and secondary schools in Victoria, Australia. Also in relation to the education system of Australia and the Pacific Islands (Solomon Islands), Carrington, in different co-authored research papers (Carrington and Duke: 2014; Carrington, Bourke and Dharan: 2012, Carrington and Elkins: 2002) proposes the use of the Index for Inclusion especially as a vehicle for developing inclusive school communities, but simultaneously highlights other issues such as the rift (in legal-bureaucratic terms) between inclusive policies and particular school cultures. This is to say, she emphasizes the gap between policy and practice (2002), the need to recognize that these are models of inclusion developed in the West from the perspective of human rights (2014), and the strong support required by education staff to review school practice focusing on the participation and learning of all students. She also points out the need for policy development to be culturally founded (2012). Again, for Queensland, Australia, a paper by Duke (2009) proposes, based on the Ainscow and Booth Index for Inclusion, an innovation for the improvement and development of a learning community in the district, with impact on the design of its curricular framework. Thus, it foresees the development of action plans arising from the consideration of the participants' expectations and the results of the learning processes they achieve, based on the values, dimensions and indicators proposed by the Index.

In turn, the work of Duran, Echeita, Giné, Miquel, Ruiz and Sandoval Mena (2005) describes the adaptation of the Index for Inclusion (based on the UNESCO translation for Latin America) for its application in Spain, particularly in the district of Madrid, through Consorcio Universitario para la Educación Inclusiva (University Consortium for Inclusive Education; and in Catalonia, carried out by the Grup de treball sobre Escola Inclusiva (Work Group on Inclusive School) of the ICE (Institute of Education Sciences) of the University of Barcelona. In the former case, the Index was applied in a secondary school in the Community of Madrid, while the Catalonian version was implemented in three schools with a very diverse student body. The study also reports on tests carried out in the Basque Country with the participation of the Basque Government's Department of Education, initially in two public schools, but with projection to a larger number of institutions. The publication concludes with an auspicious future use of the Index for Inclusion as an element of innovation and change towards a more inclusive education.

Also related to Spain, but with a different analysis proposal, the work of Sánchez, Rodríguez and Sandoval (2019) stands out: it is a descriptive study (through the application of the Index for Inclusion) on school inclusion in primary educational centers in Spain, comprising 430 professionals from different schools. The particularly interesting aspect of this study is that it sounds out what are the obstacles and the facilitators for school inclusion, and establishes the relationship between the variables usually identified in research and the degree of inclusion. Some of the variables included are: type of institution (public or private), the location (urban or rural), schools considered learning communities, number of support teachers, number of regular students and number of students with "special educational needs" (as is the category used by the authors), way of grouping students by the school, family participation, etc. In their results, they emphasize that the sociodemographic characteristics of the establishment or the type of school, as well as the number of students with a disability are not significantly related to school inclusion (i.e., they would be neutral variables). On the other hand, the existence of a greater number of support teachers is presented as a negative variable, as the greater the number of specialist teachers or therapists there is, the less inclusion is observed. Contrarily, the level of family participation raises the inclusion level records, as does the cohesion of the educational community and the expression of high expectations of teachers concerning their students. Finally, the existence of school innovation plans also have an impact on the level of inclusion and the quality of teaching.

The work of Halinen and Järvinen (2008) on inclusive education in Finland is also referenced in this section despite the fact that it does not report on levels of inclusion, the reason for this omission being -precisely- that the Finish education system adheres to full inclusion of students with disabilities and, simultaneously, very high educational quality and equity. The referred publication highlights the strong impact on the process of change in education policies brought about by the UNESCO Education for All initiatives and, in particular, by the Convention on the Rights of Persons with Disabilities, since it was through the implementation of the latter that all Finnish students of the same age receive a similar basic education, including those with more severe developmental deficiencies. The authors point out that in Finland it is commonplace to consider that pre-school and basic education is a right for all, which results in more than 99.7% of students completing the nine years of multipurpose education. In the accomplishment of said inclusion, the authors identify three fundamental, concatenated stages or steps in the Finnish system: (i) the guarantee of access to education for all, i.e., the obligation to attend school and complete at least basic studies, which is fulfilled through the effective establishment of a wide network of schools, and free tuition; (ii) the prioritization of quality improvement and the extension of the time spent in school (curriculum improvement, pedagogical training); (iii) the elimination of obstacles to learning and the provision of support. Based on the Finnish experience, the authors propose considering five "spheres of development" to achieve permanent progress in the field of inclusion: 1) that the concept of inclusive education be supported by values embraced by society; 2) that all children attend school (which implies decisions about distances between home and school); 3) that work be done with participation of all members of society on collaborative principles and with support from families; 4) strong professional capability of teachers and solid interaction with the system; 5) a curriculum that expresses the basic values of inclusive education, with open, supportive and interactive processes of analysis and evaluation, which are only possible through cooperation between administrators at different levels and jurisdictions.

As regards the possibility that the Ainscow and Booth Index for Inclusion may be a useful tool to drive greater educational inclusion, and in doing so, project it throughout a local system, the work of Heung (2006) -focused on the Hong Kong education system- is especially interesting. In her work, she develops an adaptation of the Index -thus designing the Hong Kong Indicators for Inclusion- and highlights the incidence of cultural differences in the modeling of the measurement instrument, as well as its limitations in projecting changes at scale, the school culture (and its capacity or incapacity) for self-evaluation, and its performance standards. Lastly, mention cannot be omitted of some works critical of the Index for Inclusion, in particular, those by Forlin and Loreman (2014), and Alvarez Balandra (2011). In the first referenced work, the authors conduct their research in two sections: the first one dedicated to the analysis of general and specific notions of inclusion (conceptualization on inclusive education) with definitions and concepts on evaluation, policy implementation, inclusive classrooms, the role of the teacher, resources and elimination of obstacles, to name a few. In the second section, the authors begin by raising the ethical challenges and dilemmas involved in attempting to measure inclusive education, and then review publications on the development of international indicators. The work is both relevant and ambitious in its approach; it systematizes theoretical contents and practical experiences while compiling works by different authors. The starting point is the idea that the international adoption of inclusive practices is the most equitable and global approach to education, which is, in turn, related to compliance with international declarations and conventions. Thus, recognizing the topicality and growing importance of the subject matter, the study also acknowledges the complexity and diversity of realities that present significant disparities in both the conceptualization and implementation of inclusive education. Volume 3 of this series (International Perspectives on Inclusive Education) contributes to the international academic discourse, since it goes over the various philosophies and practices whose review it proposes according to a given context, always with a view to providing assistance to those taking part in this school practice. The study provides an approach for the measurement of inclusive education, reviews its different conceptualizations, describes the ways in which each system measures or attempts to measure its impact and effectiveness, while highlighting the complexity of the problems associated with this measurement (ethical problems, problems associated with the application of models transferred from other cultural environments, policy development and implementation, teacher preparation assessment, teacher characteristics, types of leadership, etc.). The work attempts to contribute to the construction of internal markers for continuous improvement, as well as to the setting and postulation of objectives -which are usually absent or unclear-. While the first section deals mainly with the conceptualization of measurement in inclusive education, and the complexity of the problems it presents (including its practical implications), the second section is devoted to measurement in practice, and reviews the development of different indicators of inclusive education around the world.

In turn, the work of Álvarez Balandra (2011) proposes an open critique of the Index for Inclusion, not in terms of its usefulness as a measurement instrument, but rather based on the founding premises of the main schools of Action Research: the English school, whose main referents are Elliot and Stenhouse; and the Australian school, represented by Carr, Kemmis and Mac Taggart. Álvarez Balandra affirms, under the prism of action research, that the reflection generated by the teacher (on a curriculum as a flexible process of development and evaluation) is "process and product at the same time" because it occurs simultaneously in practice, and the empirical data becomes relevant and is, thus, the basis for improving practical reflection. However, (citing Elliot) the author denounces that action research "has been hijacked in the service of technical rationality" (p.6), so that teachers use it with total disregard for the ethical dimension of teaching and learning, since they use it simply as a way of controlling student learning. For this reason, the author calls for the incorporation of an ethical dimension in the Index for Inclusion. He also calls for a more prominent role for teachers, accusing Ainscow and Booth of virtually eliminating the teacher by subordinating their work to that of the coordinator who guides or drives the work of applying the Index. In this way, he argues, dialogue loses its own characteristics as a communicative action that requires a circular relationship (instrumental, strategic, conversational, rule-regulated and dramaturgical communicative action), and no longer privileges the speaker (teacher) but the listener (coordinator). He concludes that the ways to achieve greater inclusion can only be built on the specificity of each school, admitting a multiplicity of forms, but not with a pre-established general normative instrument (as is how he considers the Index).

In this section, reference has been made to the publications closest to this study on the issue of measuring and analyzing levels of school inclusion. So far, then, the more academic view; let us now move on to the monitoring of reality with a focus on the right to inclusive education and the organization of the education system in question.

3

SURVEYS CONDUCTED BY CIVIL SOCIETY ORGANIZATIONS

The United Nations Organization has committees in charge of monitoring compliance with the conventions signed by the member States, as a way of preventing international agreements from being reduced to mere declarations without practical application. Consequently, for said purpose, the UN foresees an agenda for reviewing compliance with the treaties, so that the member countries can be informed about the state of compliance and its progress with certain periodicity: the measures adopted, their implementation and the official data available. Part of this monitoring mechanism, which includes requests for information, observations and recommendations to the States, involves the participation of civil society organizations of the country in question, in order to have information derived not only from the public authorities, but also from citizen oversight that enables contrasting the official information.

As regards the Convention on the Rights of Persons with Disabilities, the Committee of the same name is the body of independent experts that supervises its implementation, and to which compliance reports are submitted (through the Secretary General of the United Nations), as provided for in the corresponding Optional Protocol. In 2017, the latest review was conducted by this Convention for Argentina, involving the presentation of various reports by the Argentine State, alliances and networks of civil society organizations (some of which based in the Province of Buenos Aires), and by the efensoría General de la Nación (Public Defender's Office).[1]

---

1 The "List of issues prior to the submittal of the combined second and third periodic report of Argentina" (i.e. the information requested by the Committee from the Argentine State) included: Education (art. 24). Please provide information disaggregated by age, sex and disability, including percentages of educational inclusion at all levels and in all regions of the member State. Please account for the number of persons with disabilities in segregated special education as compared to the number of students with disabilities in inclusive education, and the number and geographical

Though not dealing exclusively with the educational situation of the Province of Buenos Aires, the reports presented by civil society organizations are, in our opinion, fairly useful input because they contribute to understanding, on the basis of specific surveys, the situation in Argentina of persons with disabilities. Some of the reports refer only to the right to inclusive education, while others address the situation of compliance with all, or almost all, the rights recognized by the Convention. Since the subject matter of interest in this study is strictly focused on the education field, reference will be limited to this issue (contemplated in Article 24 of the Convention) and to the central aspects of the reports submitted to the UN. A total of six reports were submitted (including that of the Public Defender's Office), -with overall and partial scopes, and recommendations for the list of questions to be addressed to the State-, as reported in "United Nations treaty body databases, reporting status for Argentina" (UN, Office of the High Commissioner). In general terms, the reports denounce limited effective compliance with the right to inclusive education for the country in general, while recognizing advances in terms of regulations. They do so by making the following observations:

- They criticize the structure of the education system at the national level (Law 26206) -prior to our country adopting the Convention- and its provision for a common education system with a segregated special education subsystem for people with disabilities
- They highlight in a positive light the regulatory change introduced by Federal Education Council Resolution Number 311/2016, with the limitations derived from the need for provincial jurisdictions to introduce the resolution in its local regulations (some provinces omit the regulation of that Federal Resolution because it does not conform to the regulatory framework of the province)
- They denounce the lack of sufficient numbers of professionals assigned to educational inclusion, especially in the case of students

---

coverage of resource centers for inclusion. Please indicate the existence of reasonable adjustments in the educational environment and teacher-training programs on inclusive education. Please provide information on the resources allocated for the implementation of Resolution 311/2016 of the Federal Council of Education on the promotion, accreditation, certification and award of degrees and diplomas of students with disabilities and on programs aimed at preventing the rejection of students with disabilities in mainstream education, and creating an inclusive educational environment. Please provide information on whether General Comment No. 4 (2016) on the right to inclusive education has been recognized by the member State's public authorities. (CRPD/C/ARG/QPR/2-3).

without medical coverage, which results in the absence of inclusive vacancies in regular schools, and the consequent automatic referral to special schools at entry level, and at schooling progress milestones and changes of cycle (from pre-school, to primary, to secondary levels). That is to say, the systematic rejection of the enrollment of people with disabilities in mainstream education and mechanisms of referral to special schools based on the medical model.

- They refer to the existence of situations of abuse of power in private schools, when parents of students with disabilities are forced to sign documents that mean the waiver of the right to inclusion. In the case of the Province of Buenos Aires, the (now repealed) imposition of dual enrollment is denounced as a violation of rights and of freedom of choice.

- They highlight the lack of teacher-training programs and the allegation by teachers that they are not qualified to comply with the educational inclusion of students with disabilities. Added to this is the aggravating factor that pre-school teacher training remains structured as two separate fields, regular and special education.

- They point out the disparity between the information collected for regular schools and special education schools (they denounce the lack of data regarding students attending special schools, their learning levels, their educational trajectories).

- They denounce the lack of physical and communicational accessibility in schools, the lack of mechanisms for the resolution of school conflicts related to inclusion and the scarce participation of people with disabilities in the definition of public policies. They report the existence of legal claims for the violation of rights.

The aforementioned works constitute the core of reports presented in 2017 at international level, and the present study takes into account that, as the Province of Buenos Aires is the place of residence of 40% of the total school population of Argentina, what is stated therein is reasonably applicable to the entire school environment of the Province of Buenos Aires. However, it is worth mentioning that -as seen in the section corresponding to that particular education system-, at a later date than the reports referenced herein were produced, important advances were made in the Province of Buenos Aires -from a normative standpoint- towards the recognition and the implementation of inclusive education.

4

THEORETICAL FRAMEWORK

The issue of inclusive education involves such an ample variety of vital aspects that it becomes extremely difficult to delimit. While in the introduction of this work certain boundaries are established and basic concepts defined -or rather, there is an acknowledgement of the meaning assigned herein to the indeterminate notions of inclusion, disability and inclusive education-, omitting a review of other issues would not only greatly impoverish this analysis, but would also imply a corseted presentation of a challenging reality that requires thoughtful elaboration

4.1. EDUCABILITY, SCHOOL AND SCHOOL FAILURE

Already at the dawn of the foundation of expert knowledge that was later to become pedagogy, educators Jan Comenius in his Didactica Magna of 1632 and Jean Baptiste de La Salle in his Meditations on the Mystery of Teaching and in The Guide for Christian Schools of 1706 raised the questions about whom to educate. Who does the teacher address? Who is the passive subject of the act of educating? Who is to be educated and how? Who is the school for? All questions aimed at designing a teaching method capable of being replicated and applied on a larger scale. Thus, in trying to establish the primal material, that with which the school works (the child), a concept was outlined that was later developed as the principle of universal educability, which postulates that everyone should be educated, for only in this way can a creature born as a basic man, closer to the material world than to transcendental life, become that he is meant to be: a Man in every sense of the word. "God wants all men to come to the knowledge of truth and wants all to be saved" (De La Salle, n.d.1951: p. 2). "All those who are born men require teaching, because it is necessary that they be men, not ferocious beasts, not brutes, not inert trunks" (Comenius, 1998, p. 17). "God himself always assures us that before him there is no concept of persons" (p.22)

It is evident that behind - or rather, as the very foundation of - the principle of universal educability, there lies a particular notion of man and, consequently, of education and of school. The child is not merely an intellectual or functional being, but a whole, and this is also how school is conceived. This pansophical ideal that proposes teaching everything to everyone is, thus, intimately linked to the concept of public school (Narodowski, 2018). In line with Simons and Masschelein (2014), this school represents, precisely, the window to the world.

> It is a democratic intervention in the sense that it "creates" free time for all, regardless of origin and, precisely because of this, it instates equality. School is an invention that turns everyone into a student and, in that sense, puts everyone in the same initial situation. At school, the world becomes public. Therefore, it has nothing to do with initiation into the culture or lifestyle of a particular group (of a social position, a class, etc.). With the invention of the school, society offers the opportunity for a new beginning, a renewal. (p. 96)

Starting from this theoretical framework that admits universal educability, and that sees the school as a space of vital opportunity (Simons and Masschelein, 2014), this study will reflect on the education of students with disabilities: the education of all will only be possible if what must be transmitted can be received and processed by all. The core of knowledge will be adapted on the basis of those essential capabilities of the student that are considered vital for their development as a person. "In schools, everything should be taught to everyone", Comenius points out, but clarifies that this does not imply deeming it is necessary for everyone to have knowledge of all the sciences and arts (p. 24). De La Salle (n.d. 1951) also alludes, in a certain way, to the need to adapt, by stipulating that pupils should be taught what they should know according to their age and capability, and without neglecting the most ignorant or the poorest. Nowadays, it is argued that the school can and should not be a mere transmitter of data and information, but should rather work on the development of students' competencies: the ability to solve problems with autonomy, to learn throughout life, to communicate and interact, to listen to and include others, to tolerate uncertainty, among others things. There are even those who argue (Aldrich, 2011) -in line with the home schooling movement- that education today requires unschooling rules, so that education encompasses three vital aspects: learning to be (through self-reflection), learning to do (which implies a lot of practice), and learning to know (focused on knowledge concentrated in books and lessons). The study of educability itself -as already stated with regard to disability- is a matter of such importance that it would also merit a separate paper, which is why this study is limited to only some of its facets: educability takes on a sociological aspect (Flude and Ahier, 2013; Bernstein, 2000), while behavior also gains relevance. This brief recount of works on this topic cannot fail to include that of Rutter, Tizard and Whitmore (1970).

The debate on the pedagogical aspects of inclusive education shines the spotlight on the difference between the pedagogy of deviation/deviance and the pedagogy of inclusion. The former establishes a hierarchy of cognitive aptitudes to measure a student's ability, explains school failure in terms of learning difficulties derived from the student's deficiency, focuses school responses on deficiencies, accentuates specialization as the core competence of teachers, and proposes an alternative curriculum for underachieving students; the pedagogy of inclusion, on the other hand, emphasizes the learning potential of each student, argues that school failure is related to insufficient responses on the part of the school, stresses the need for active participation of students in the learning process, and postulates the need for a common curriculum for all students (Opertti and Belalcázar, 2008). Along the same lines, on the question of whether it is possible to educate children with disabilities, it is interesting to note that other authors (Baquero and Narodowski: 1991, Skliar: 2007, 2005; Ainscow: 2007) also point out that, in the face of failure, the adverse result is rarely attributed to the method used or to the teacher's skills; failure is always due to and belongs to the student. Even in the field of special schools, psychologists tend to analyze the problem from a "reduction to the individual", overlooking an examination of the educational situation. This is the reality denounced by Tomlinson when she proposes a sociological analysis of education. The derivations, and even the evaluations by psychologists in the form of reports, tests and grids, are far removed from the school situation. However, is the student with a disability really the only one to blame for their school failure?

Valdez (2012) holds that the configuration of the educability criterion is especially linked to the complexity of teaching knowledge and practices, and to the school's own evaluation practices. In other words, the child might not seem to be the problem -or at least, not the only problem-, nor is the teacher. According to this author, the problem of educability derives from the school setting or environment; it is necessary to re-contextualize practices in order to avoid reducing the problem to an individual (student or teacher), and thus analyze the phenomenon in its true complexity within the school system (p. 51). The complexity of the phenomenon of school failure might seem to refer to the teaching situation, and also to the way in which inclusion is managed (i.e., the institutional policy and the implementation of said policy). In Tomlinson's terms, the phenomenon must be related to the type of school of the 20th century, economically competitive societies and their workforce, the curriculum proposed at the political level, and the permanent shift in educational standards in line with competition, competitiveness between teachers in terms of their teaching careers, the efficiency of their work, etc. (2012; 2014). Perrenoud (1990; 2004; 2005) also describes school success, failure, and inequalities as constructed realities, while proposing "ten new competencies for teaching". The questioning of educability, the pathologization of the student and school failure find a way out in Carlos Skliar's concept of otherness, according to which education is no more (and no less) than the place of the relationship of the encounter with the other (Skliar and Larrosa, 2009). Alternatively, from another very different perspective, it also finds a way out in the compensatory function of the school, in an attempt to alleviate unequal development, given the differences that result from different forms of marginalization (Litwin, 1994).

4.2. DISABILITY AND ITS DENOMINATIONS

As stated when the problem was presented, the concept of disability has undergone a series of modifications, changing from what was known as the medical model to the social model. The medical model associates disability, that is to say the person's deficit, with the medical diagnosis of the specialist who establishes what disease, syndrome or handicap the person suffers from per se, independently of their environment. On the other hand, the social notion of disability assigns to the environment a relevant role in the impairments of the person, which thus cease to be deemed inherent to "the person". The person no longer "suffers" from a disability, nor "is disabled", but faces an environment that limits their abilities by not lifting the social, physical and/or access obstacles to include them in all activities of their life. The focus is first placed on the person -not on their deficit or diagnosis-, and then their limitations appear, directly linked to the environment (Portuondo Sao, 2004; Buitrago Echeverri and Lara Bernal, 2013; Torres González, 2010; Maldonado, 2013).

The definition of disability that will be adopted for this research draws on both, and is contained in the preamble of the International Convention on the Rights of Persons with Disabilities (UN, 2006) which in its section e) reads:

> Recognizing that disability is an evolving concept and that disability results from the interaction between persons with impairments and attitudinal and environmental obstacles that hinder their full and effective participation in society on an equal basis with others.

When this concept of disability is adopted, its mere mention does not imply contempt or discrimination, but only the description of a situation of disadvantage in the face of an environment that does not contribute to personal development. Thus, the substitution of the word disability by the extended expression special educational needs (SEN) will not be embraced. This expression is not only beset with the inadequacy of any euphemism, but -in line with Tomlinson- is a construction developed within the interaction between professionals, therapists and members of the State (administrative bureaucracy) to expand the boundaries of special education, so that it can justifiably receive all types of students, who do not necessarily have a disability or deficit; these are simply children who fail to meet the (increasingly higher) standards set forth as objectives in modern societies, be it due to their social, cultural, or economic environment, to a personal limitation, whether permanent or transient, or to the existing neurodiversity. In this sense, Armstrong (2012a) proposes to abandon the approach to the study of disability as a disorder and suggests the concept of neurodiversity, leading to a proposal for a new school approach. Ainscow and Booth also reject the concept of SEN, and, when alluding to the need to develop a language for inclusion, explain that the approach associated with this concept has limitations as a model for resolving educational difficulties and can be an obstacle for the development of inclusive practices in schools. This occurs because labeling a student with SEN generates lower expectations on the part of teachers, and also because this practice focuses on the difficulties experienced by labeled students. Thus, in short, it tends to reinforce in teachers the belief that the education of students in their classrooms classified as having SEN is primarily the responsibility of a specialist (Ainscow and Booth, 2002a).

On a different note, it should be highlighted that the obsession to avoid labeling is often a double-edged sword (Valdez, 2012): though it is done to avoid stigmatization and the consequent limitation of labels that prevent those students from experiencing, discovering and developing their individual potentialities, the lack of diagnosis leads to ignorance and uncertainty, resulting in the lack of development of tools and support for students' learning and for their permanence in school. The work of Filidoro (2011) is particularly relevant when the contradiction is discussed between the pathologization of the label and the usefulness of an appropriate diagnosis, insofar as it denounces (in line with the Sociology of Special Education) that psycho-pedagogy is often conducive to the certification of the impossibility of learning, the identification of the non-educable to consummate the very same operation of exclusion. This is the trap exposed by Benasayag and Schmit (2010), between helping patients in their "cure" (i.e. schooling them to educate and socialize them) and, simultaneously, relieving society of the discomfort of those who do not adapt to the ideal of social functioning (by way of their segregation in special schools).

4.3. SCHOOL MANAGEMENT, CHANGE AND LEADERSHIP

School and society used to be quite different, which poses new challenges. Although school grammar remains the same and the Comenian principle of systemic simultaneity still governs school dynamics, new forms of socialization, the change or end of childhood (Postman, 1994; Baquero and Narodowski, 1994), the metamorphosis of the family (Romero, 2004), the modification of the terms of its partnership with the school, and the phenomenon of a global pandemic have ushered in a new school reality (Narodowski, 1999). The world is now different from the one in which the school was born, and so are its dynamics, social and family relationships. We have crossed several "divides" and are facing "new realities", in Drucker's terms (2011). As Aldrich proposes, the only sustainable response to meet the global educational challenge is to adopt a diversity of perspectives (2011).

The concept of school management understood as control and administration, typical of bureaucracy, was replaced by management exerted as government or articulation of interests, to finally define management as gesta (Latin for "deeds" or "acts"): the project is now the school itself, and its central problems are, today, inequality and quality: "management unfolds within the territory of possibility, of what is to come, by transforming the given into new possibilities" (Romero, 2013: p. 12). The understanding of how schools change (or remain the same), and therefore of the limits and practical possibilities of their development, must consider intra-organizational processes, particularly so if a more egalitarian, fair and effective education is to be achieved (Ball, 1994). This is the challenge.

In order to elucidate it, it is interesting to see the work of Skliar (2005), who tries to detect, with respect to inclusive education, which of the arguments of pedagogy have remained intact in spite of the changes of the school; he identifies three of them: the argument of completeness (the existence of the school is justified because the student is an incomplete or limited being, who must be completed), the argument of the future (childhood is thought of as a temporality), and the argument of a logic of explanation and understanding (the role of the explainer or teacher is only justified because the incapable person who needs the explanation was created previously). Skliar confronts these arguments with those that seem to delineate the school of today's prefigurative society (Mead, 2006) and its childhood: the argument of difference, of concern for the other, of tolerance and respect for diversity and, ultimately, of educational inclusion. Moreover, he concludes boldly: "there is no such thing as 'special education', but a disciplinary invention created by the idea of 'normality' to introduce order into the disorder originated by the disturbance of that other invention we call 'abnormality' (2005: p. 4). There exists a dispute for the perpetuation or implosion of traditional special education (special modality, for students outside the "normal"), which should now be thought of as a discourse that destroys the idea of normality, a category that is expelled from inclusive education.

It will then have to be analyzed to what extent schools in the education system of the Province of Buenos Aires are enabling spaces that build bridges and eliminate obstacles for the full inclusion of children, to what extent they develop inclusion policies, and how these are made effective in practice. To evaluate whether it is possible -or rather, whether it will be possible- no longer to describe schools as normal, special or simply inclusive. On this issue, Ainscow (2007) proposes the inclusive school as a real challenge. This new inclusive school is no longer designed exclusively by political-pedagogues; rather, following Fullan (1993), a fundamental change in the way of thinking about educational change is needed to solve the basic and insurmountable problem of the juxtaposition of continuous change with clearly conservative education systems. This author explains that current times are characterized, on the one hand, by the constant and expansive presence of innovation and education reform (to such an extent that dealing with change has become an endemic phenomenon of postmodern society); but, on the other hand and simultaneously, education systems are fundamentally conservative (in the training of teachers, school organization, their own hierarchies, and even in the way decisions are made by those who define public policies). For this reason, the author postulates the need to transform education systems into "learning" organizations that take change and innovation in their stride as part of their regular work, no longer in so far as education policy guidelines and reforms are concerned, but as a true way of life. And this urgency to develop learning organizations is based on the lack of certainties presented by the world - in general terms, not only in schools -, a world that has become complex (even chaotic), full of uncertainties, paradoxes and tensions, and even contradictions (care and attention vs. competition, equity vs. excellence) that must be reconciled and reconverted into potential for growth and development, because the society of the 21st century requires citizens capable of relating to change proactively throughout their lives, both individually and collaboratively in a global context of dynamic multicultural transformation (Fullan, 1993). This requires not only the recognition of change, but also the construction of knowledge that is shared (without losing sight of its moral purpose), learning in context, the development of interpersonal relationships and coherence (with personal and common commitment directed towards specific objectives and through defined courses of action). However, fundamentally, it also calls for a new form of leadership, less hierarchical, of a distributed nature, which can no longer radiate from top down, but that is nourished by the day-to-day nature of organizational behavior. This is only possible with the presence of several leaders (Fullan, 2001).

If we think about the specific scenario of school micro-politics and the leadership styles identified by Ball (2012) -interpersonal, managerial, political-confrontational and political-authoritarian types of leadership-, none of them would seem to be up to the new reality. While interpersonal leadership vindicates teamwork, the development of autonomy and the sense of trust and obligation through informal communications, it presents a personalist face that results in loyalty being developed towards the person of the principal rather than towards the school (the author compares it to the feudal regime); managerial leadership implies the professionalization of the team and the definition of purposes and objectives that will allow an objective evaluation of performance, but is based on a formal structure of bureaucratic-type procedures that, much though it fosters a sense of organizational responsibility (non-personalist), results in the exclusion of teachers from relevant discussions and decisions, which are then limited to the technical advisory team. As for confrontational political leadership, with emphasis on dialogue scenarios that enable controversy, although it presents discussion spaces for decision making and enables the recognition of different interests and ideologies within the school, it is still but a political-theatrical skirmish that causes disinterest and frustration in part of the team in the face of the futility of supposed debates carried out in foreign territory and directed towards pre-established positions. The phenomenon is similar in organizations with political-authoritarian leadership, although in these organizations, the leader, far from being geared towards change, clings to the statu quo and defends the policies and procedures of the institution. Today's world requires new leadership. Today's world requires leaders of integrity, who share their authority for the creation of a shared vision, who build trust on truth, who show themselves as willing to serve rather than as winners, who share time with their teams and achieve collaborative work that drives the organization towards the achievement of its objectives, thanks to the sense of belonging and security of each member (Sinek, 2014).

However, the present research is focused on an education system, so although it is of interest to review the development, transformation and renewal of leadership types in general and of school leadership in particular -linked to change or innovation-, it is also limited because its scope of influence is restricted to the life of the organization or school in question. It is indeed necessary to think of a type of leadership with greater impact, a systemic type of leadership as proposed by Hopkins. In his work Realizing the potential of system leadership, which is part of the OECD dossier on Improving School Leadership, 2008, the author argues that it is this type of leadership (systemic leadership) that can lead to sustainable transformation of education, and defines this leader as a principal who is concerned about and works for the success of other schools as much as for the success of their own. The author characterizes this systemic leadership as imbued with a moral purpose that can be expressed in various ways (among them: measuring its success in terms of learning and narrowing gaps, committing to personalized education, conceiving schools as learning communities, focusing on greater equity and inclusion through interventions in the context and culture, etc.), and which offers a variety of roles: the development of joint improvement of education by several schools, school improvement in particularly challenging circumstances, the development of community networks, among others. This leadership implies, in any case, some adaptive work with four vital functions: setting a direction or objective, management of teaching and learning, development of students and teachers, and growth of the organization. Building on this characterization of systemic leadership and its domains, the author proposes the following principles for large-scale improvement: (a) maintaining an instructional focus over time (and applying it to all members of the organization); (b) incorporating into the routine accountability for practices and performance; (c) reducing isolation and opening practices to direct observation, analysis and critique; (d) providing differentiated treatment based on performance and capability; (e) delegating greater discretion. It would seem, however, and in spite of the above, that in order to think about educational change on a large scale, it may not be enough to reformulate leadership towards "leadership for inclusion" (Ainscow and Miles, 2008) and the construction of "systemic leadership" (Hopkins, 2008).

It seems necessary to include other issues, such as the consideration of the peculiar content of policy formulation and decision-making -a scenario where there participate other variables of "choice and exit" on the part of families (Di John, 2007)-, given that much of it is of ideological origin, and consequently, its debate and discussion are frequently exposed in terms of equity and fairness (Ball, 2012). Decision-making in the design and implementation of education policies also appears to be limited or surrounded by the current situation and the weight acquired by other factors: electoral times, budgetary restrictions, teacher bargaining negotiations and even the school calendar impose their own pace on the dynamics in a province where teachers' salaries account for 97% of the education budget and what is urgent postpones the -also urgent- debate on the quality of education (see Sánchez Zinny, 2020). In addition to the difficulty of the timing and pace imposed by the political reality, by the strength of unions and by the school cycle, there are the paradoxes present in the Buenos Aires scenario. In the present times, besides, to all this should be added the difficulties caused by a global pandemic and mass school closures in the Province of Buenos

Aires. The paradox, for example, of the expansion of school coverage in coexistence with growing economic-labor exclusion, all of which is part of the current scenario that imposes for some, among other things, the need to rethink the competencies of secondary education in order to narrow the gap between the worlds of school and of labor (Clucellas and Scaliter, 2011). This and other contradictions or paradoxes are particularly and painfully evident in the scenario that is the special object of this research: the education system of the Province of Buenos Aires. This is what Gorostiaga, Acedo and González (2004) and Adrogué (2013) point out for different levels and cycles, and at different times. Both works expose in different ways and with different approaches the paradox of inclusion-exclusion, universalization-quality education, and show the need to articulate other ways to solve the phenomenon of educational exclusion (due to lack of access, school repetition or dropping out) and low educational outcomes in terms of quality. While the first work focuses on the study of the implementation process of the 1993 education reform in the secondary schools of the Province of Buenos Aires (third cycle of the General Basic School) and describes the phenomenon of a province whose population, geography and education system have their own characteristics, the second research focuses on primary schools throughout the country and the need to review quality of education and its "distribution" (or horizontal equity) through the application of three indices that take into account the psychic, human and social dimensions of the schools; among its results, it reveals that the Province of Buenos Aires ranks amongst the worst equity scenarios. Unfortunately, this reality is painfully exacerbated as a consequence of the effects of the COVID pandemic ravaging the region.

4.4. EDUCATION SYSTEM (AND SCHOOL CULTURE)

In order to conceptualize and characterize education systems (it should be remembered that this study attempts to measure the level of inclusion of a system, not of a school or a particular group of educational institutions) the perspective of Viñao (2002) will be followed, from whose approach it is worth highlighting the permanent and active linkage, the play and interaction -it might be called vital- that he proposes between education systems, school cultures and changes. This is so because the purpose of the Index is none other than to set in motion a process of change, which brings school culture into the limelight.

It seems difficult, from this approach, to understand an education system from a static or strictly bureaucratic-legalistic point of view, or even to try to define an education system without taking into account school cultures and reforms. Here, system and culture appear as linked. It is from this perspective that the author begins by answering the question (recurrent almost to exhaustion in the academic world dedicated to education) as to whether we are witnessing the end of education systems, basically due to their displacement in the face of phenomena such as the new forms of teaching brought about by technology, the replacement of forms of socialization (no longer only schooling in childhood), the dissemination of knowledge (now available on the networks), and the displacement of the provision of education services due to their decentralization, globalization and/or privatization. To these phenomena, we can now add the global pandemic caused by the COVID virus, with the very strong implications that the closure of educational institutions at all levels has brought about, and whose consequences are still unknown. The answer to this question is blunt and negative: social transformations, greater territorial diversity or even the privatization of education not only do not jeopardize the existence of the education system in the strict sense or "school system", but it is precisely their existence that makes it possible to achieve the objectives of education policies by changing the role played by the State and assigning some functions to private agencies or bodies outside the formal education system. It is here that the distinction between school institution and school form becomes most important, since (according to Viñao, 2002) we are actually facing the adoption of school forms on the part of non-school educational agencies, which do not acquire or implement them as one more alternative among other possible ones but, on the contrary, as "the only possible and legitimate ways of socially configuring educational activities" (p. 6). The phenomenon is, then, that of the expansion of school forms with increasing force and to different spheres (including the family), so that far from being the end of education systems, we are witnessing their transformation and the reinforcement of some of their typical characteristics and functions, such as horizontal and vertical segmentation.

Viñao explains that the formation of education systems entails an intentional or sought-after process (with purposes on the part of those who promote them) that, depending on the country, requires shorter or more prolonged periods of time, and goes through different phases until it is configured and consolidated, and that frequently includes effects different from those that were intended by those who devised them.

> National education systems imply the existence of a network or set of formal educational institutions: a) differentiated by levels or cycles and interrelated; b) managed, supervised or controlled by public agencies and agents; c) financed, at least in part, by one or some of the public administrations; d) run by teachers trained, selected or supervised by these agents and paid in whole or in part from a public budget; and e) that issue certifications or credentials regulated in terms of their formal validity and issuance by the public authorities. (Viñao, 2002, p. 9).

In accordance with the above characterization, the following elements are typical of the process of configuration of the system: (1) considering education as a matter of competence of the public authority; (2) transferring functions to public agencies as well as their control or inspection of educational institutions; (3) configuring an administration of management, execution and inspection; (4) setting of certain contents, methods, disciplines and modes of organization by the public authorities (through curricula and other regulations); (5) professionalization of public sector teachers (requirement of a diploma, appointment and payment by public agencies, training academies, etc.); (6) configuration of a network of schools according to uniform criteria though entailing classifications, differentiations and hierarchies (by curricula and target groups) with the aim of reaching the entire child and adolescent population. The growing existence of various decentralization programs from the central administration to schools, which, although mainly financial, involves management issues or resources inherent to school life (e.g. teachers, buildings), does not jeopardize the existence of the system, but rather it is the system which (through federal initiatives, state or even municipal programs) redesigns new forms that aspire to greater economic efficiency and simultaneous improvement in the quality of education. In this regard, it is interesting to see the work of Souto Simão, Águila Mendizábal, Alas Solís, Camargo, Castillo Aramburu, Martínez Ellsbergy Villalobos Dintrans (2016) that relays different cases of decentralization programs in Latin American countries and provides detailed and systematized information about them.

Returning to Viñao (2002) and beyond the theoretical characterization given (for the purpose of providing a conceptual framework to the issue of education systems in general), what is particularly appealing in this author's analysis is his description of the processes of systematization and segmentation (internal articulation and vertical and horizontal differentiation) in relation to "the succession of expansive and inclusive waves" in turn accompanied by "restrictive and selective movements" (2002, p. 38). He explains:

> In a certain sense, the entire history of education levels and forms of education in the nineteenth and twentieth centuries can be traced back to the transition -and the consequences of this transition- from partial inclusion and, therefore, the non-schooling and exclusion of part of the population, to the simultaneous presence of more or less generalized inclusion processes over time, accompanied by processes of exclusion and compensatory expansion of other parts of the system; that is, processes of differentiation or segmentation that imply exclusion from certain trajectories or modalities and inclusion in others. (2002, p. 37).

The process of inclusion is, as he explains, the education version of the welfare state, and school culture is not a direct consequence of the process of configuration of the education system, but presents relative autonomy, since the school adapts, transforms and creates its own knowledge and culture. It is the daily reality of schools, the rituals of school life, the forms of evaluation, the structure of lessons and classes: the inertias, ideas, habits, ways of thinking and acting sedimented in schools and shared by their participants. The main participants of school culture are the teachers, but also parents, students and administrative personnel; and the central aspects of school culture are determined by these participants, the discourses, forms of communication and language, institutional and organizational aspects such as educational practices, classification of students, hierarchization of disciplines, among others. In short, as will be seen in the following sections, this conceptualization of education systems, reforms, conflicts and setbacks, and school cultures, is fully consistent with the specific theoretical framework of the present research: the dimensions proposed by Ainscow and Booth (school practices, cultures, and policies) and the dysfunctions, tensions, and conflicts - often determined by corporate interests - that bias certain education policies or forms, as Sally Tomlinson will also explain.

4.5. INSPECTORS AND SUPERVISORY SYSTEMS

The figure of the inspector, as well as supervisory systems in general, have been the subject of study and characterization in different types of publications and even in very interesting comparative studies (the McKinsey report cannot be omitted: Barber and Mourshed, 2007). Their impact on education inequality issues has also been studied according to the social environment in question as well as their interaction with other socio-educational players (De Grawe, 2008). Unfortunately, the framework of this research does not make it possible to go further into the issue, to review typified inspection and/or supervision models, or even those proposed to address the different dimensions (De Grauwe and Carron, 2007), or to present comparatively some national systems (in this regard, see Terigi, 2009).

However, it is worth mentioning some issues briefly, especially those related to the role of the inspector in the management of public policies and in school improvement processes, a phenomenon that has increasingly been securing a place for itself in the educational agenda, especially in the face of the current paradoxical process in which there coexist, on the one hand, the tendency to deregulate and provide greater school autonomy, and, on the other hand, the strengthening of the State's control function. It would seem that -even in spite of the progressive flexibilization of supervisory systems as they were known in the past- the greatest obstacle to the success of policies lies in management, i.e., in the implementation phase, much more so than in their design. It is here, then, that attention is once again focused on the role of inspectors and supervisors, emphasizing the need to develop a mediating layer whose task is performed by the body of inspectors and includes not only control, but also support and liaison. The performance of this task involves several tensions: politicization vs. professionalization, administrative focus versus pedagogy, control versus counseling (Aguerrondo, 2013). Regarding the impact of inspectors on school improvement, it is particularly interesting to see the research of Ehren and Visscher (2006) and their proposal of a theoretical model that combines the relationships between working methods in supervision, school reactions and effects (direct and collateral). In this work, the authors propose two different strategies depending on whether the schools are innovative or not.

To the functions traditionally assigned in different countries to their inspection systems (oversight functions or representation of the state in monitoring schools, support and guidance to teachers and schools towards improvement, and liaison between the central and school levels) is added a socio-community function which, in the words of Terigi, "refers to the role of inspectors in promoting education in the social environment in which schools are established and in strengthening the relationship between families and schools" (2009, p. 57). Beyond, then, the basic tension between assistance and control, the supervisor is considered a catalyst of the education system, a dynamic force within schools, an organizational facilitator (Gvirtz and Podestá, 2012), or a hinge between the macro and the micro aspects of the education system.[1]

The above does not imply denying the difficulties that arise when one tries to grasp or outline the figure and describe the role and performance of inspectors or intermediate participants, a difficulty due -to a large extent- to the resistance and zeal of these agents with respect to information concerning their own performance. As Dufour (2007)

---

[1] On the evolution of the profession of inspector, the trend towards its professionalization, specialization and diversification, and the tensions inherent to this profession, see Viñao, 1999.

explains, when inspectors are interviewed, it is difficult to inquire about what these participants actually do, questions will rather be limited to what inspectors themselves say they do. And therefore, the work is ultimately restricted to the realm of perceptions. Hence, it is to be emphasized here that the diagnosis presented in this paper is from the perspective of inspectors.

4.6. THE SOCIOLOGICAL APPROACH TO SPECIAL EDUCATION, ACCORDING TO SALLY TOMLINSON

Despite having been initially proposed by this author in the 1980s, then expanded, further developed (2012) and consolidated during the following decades in multiple research papers (collected in Tomlinson, 2014), this approach is as innovative as it is valid: the urgent need for a sociological approach to the study of special education, so as to uncover its logic, its dynamics, the interaction of its participants and their particular interests, its link with reality and with the social structure; in short: its justification.

In her work A Sociology of special education, as well as in many other articles of her authorship (selected and compiled in The politics of race, class and special education, 2014), Tomlinson proposes to broaden the debate on Special Education through the introduction of a sociological perspective (hitherto absent) that balances the weight of the dominant approaches: medical, psychological, administrative-educational and prescriptive-educational. Aware of the innovative nature of her proposal (a sort of "denunciation"), she warns that a sociological approach is probably not only unwelcome, but possibly disturbing. And it is.

Tomlinson begins her justification of the need for the development of a true sociology of special education by pointing out that although special education is presented as imbued with an ideology of benevolent humanitarianism, this does not correspond to its historical origin, much though it served as an acceptable moral framework for the performance of professionals and practitioners of this modality, participants with personal interests in the expansion of special education, and the development of a sociology of special education.

Tomlinson highlights -and qualifies it as a "crucial" and distinctive factor- a double circumstance of this modality: that students who receive special education are not considered interlocutors (they are not considered able to speak for themselves) and that their parents have minimal intervention in school learning processes, even in spite of their growth as a pressure factor in group terms.

Thus, the author reviews the regulations issued in the United Kingdom from the very beginnings (opening of the Academy for the Deaf and Dumb in Edinburgh, in 1760), their proliferation and profusion, including the Warnock report (1978), until 1981, the International Year of the Disabled, when the "1981 Education Act" was passed, which established that: "For the purposes of this Act a child has "special educational needs" if he has a learning difficulty which calls for special educational provision to be made for him: Preliminary, (1). Certainly tautological. Already two years before the report, the number of children in state special schools was 180,000 and 15,774,774 in non-state special schools. Tomlinson describes the publication of the Warnock Report as the major event in special education during the 1970s: while presenting special education as a variant of regular education and rejecting any stigmatization of the special school, it recommended the expansion of the special school system and the revision of legal categories, so that 1 in 5 children (20% of the school population) would need, at some point in their schooling, to receive some form of special education. Thus, the legal category of disability was abolished and replaced by the more comprehensive concept of "special educational needs" accompanied by the relevant descriptive label for each child, most of whom belonged to working class families. Tomlinson discusses the number of students and the steady growth of special education enrollment, the wide scope and diversity of diagnoses, as well as the relationship between the diagnoses and the social status of the students' families. But, gradually, the type of education that was born to attend to sensory (deaf, blind children) or severe intellectual deficiencies (dumb) emerged as the type of education suitable for children who found it difficult to concentrate or were considered slow, and finally for all those who by definition were considered troublesome or problematic in regular schools. In this identification and derivation, psychology became the "classifying" discipline, inscribed in a society that, in terms of structural-functionalist sociology, might be described as focused on social order and balance, concerned with the employability of people with disabilities.

The author reviews the history of special education in England and indicates that its origins remain diffuse, possibly because of the absence of research resulting from the difficulty of probing or questioning the powerful ideology of benevolent humanitarianism, which still continues to motivate governments, professionals and other participants to identify more and more children as needing special education. But the origin of special education as a charitable deed could only have taken place at its inception - as a voluntary individual enterprise - in the same way as ordinary education did, initiated in England by the Anglican Church. Its expansion was the result of government intervention, a regulatory framework, and general development and establishment, so that the forms taken by special education result from the interplay of particular interests within society, a power struggle between doctors, psychologists and teachers, all interested in dominating the definition and domains of special education. And this power struggle cannot be dissociated (it never is) from the values and worldview of participants. The treatment given to those who are socially considered defective or handicapped depends on the values and interests of the dominant groups: in the case of England, the need for the development of an industrial society and, to this end, the employability of its population. The above implies making explicit the relationships that occur in the societies of the global knowledge economy: the interplay between education policies, the organization of education and often its "training", the pushing up of the standards of performance and qualifications of students, taking them from basic contents to levels of proficiency that are attainable only to some sectors of the population. In other words, a new idea of education that is more in line with the Human Capital theory and development according to the growth standards of modern societies and that, at the same time, must balance human rights and social justice claims that call for the inclusion of disadvantaged minorities. It is thus, then, that Special Education is provided both in segregated schools and in the general education system, all based on the medical model (whose experts identify each "pathology"), without achieving a universal type of education that welcomes the diversity of all students (see especially Tomlinson, The irresistible rise of the SEN Industry, in 2014, 55- 73; Armstrong, 2012a, b, c, 2013).

The author proposes five main questions to reveal issues that until then seemed denied or unutterable when discussing Special Education: (1) In whose interest(s) is special education currently being developed? (2) Why was there a complex development of disability categories and selection processes, how were these processes legitimized, and why, after the development of these exclusion mechanisms, is integration into general education being debated? (3) How is the special education management system linked to the use of professional expertise? Are there vested interests of growing groups of professionals who benefit from the detection of more and more students with "special educational needs"? (4) What are the goals of special education and why is the theory about its curriculum and practice insufficiently developed? (5) Are some types of special schooling more like a form of particular control of groups of children with special needs? Why is there a higher proportion of black children with special educational needs? (6) What are the goals of the expansion of special education?

In short, Tomlinson's Sociology of Special Education theory proposes, from a structural-conflict focused perspective, an analysis of special education that is willing to recognize the interest groups, identify the power and resources involved, evidence the beliefs, ideologies and rationalization processes used by agents for the legitimization of their practices, and the way in which they project effects on the -certainly weak- target of special education: children and families. The education of students with "special educational needs" ceases to be a strictly education field and becomes the domain of complex teams of therapists from various disciplines (Warnock, 1979), which, added to the influence of teachers, often results in the exclusion of parents and families. The author of the Warnock report herself explains in her brief publication:

> "As soon as a handicap is identified the local Education Service must be brought into the discussion of the child's future. Only so can parents, for their part, have any confidence in a unified and coherent body of advisers and helpers all working towards a single end, the Improvement of the prospects of a child. The

teaching profession itself has, of course, a great deal to do. The training it provides for students must be less philosophical and theoretical, more concerned with identifying needs, adapting the curriculum, coherent and conscientious keeping of records, and communication with parents. Only so will teachers become fit partners in the interdisciplinary teams that must access the needs and specify the provision for handicapped children. Local authorities, too, must be required to organize their advisory service and their supply of peripatetic teachers so that they know where the areas of greatest need are and can supply the support that is demanded."

The above, together with the exponential growth of diagnoses of students with special needs, is what motivates and prompts the formulation of the theory of the Sociology of special Education by Tomlinson. Although this researcher has been criticized in political-academic spheres -being attributed a neo-Marxist perspective by the author of the Warnock report (Tomlinson, 2014, p. 4)-, for the purposes of this research, her approach can be deemed extremely interesting and especially useful as a compass to help relate the answers provided by the members of the education system of the Province of Buenos Aires (Inspectorate-General) with their own position within it. The sociological approach will, then, make it possible to ponder, following Ainscow and Booth, on the view (and its possible biases) of each of the teachers and professionals that answered the present survey. Moreover, it does not seem to be a coincidence that these researchers also find in the field of special education a set of professional interests that prompts them to express the impossibility of redefining the field of inclusive education from within: those who come from the field of special education tend to conceive Inclusive Education as the new name for Special Education, without delving any further into the deeper phenomenon of the processes of school inclusion and exclusion (Booth and Ainscow, 1998).

4.7 MEL AINSCOW AND TONY BOOTH'S INDEX FOR INCLUSION

From a more practical standpoint geared towards the concrete generation of change processes that favor greater educational inclusion, professors Mel Ainscow and Tony Booth developed an inclusion index or Index for Inclusion (hereinafter "the Index"): this was a three-year project carried out in England by a team of teachers, parents, school board members, researchers and a representative of disability associations, under the direction of the professionals mentioned above. Between 1997 and 1998, a pilot test was carried out in six primary and secondary schools in England, from which experience a second version of the Index was developed and evaluated in 17 schools in England in the 1998-1999 school year. Since then, the Index has been progressively applied in educational institutions in different regions and countries around the world, having established itself as an accepted tool for managing institutional change towards increasing levels of inclusion.

The Index is a set of tools designed to support schools in the process of moving towards inclusive schools, taking into account the views of the teaching staff, school board members, students, families and other members of the community. These tools aim to improve educational achievement through inclusive practices. The process of working with the Index itself is designed to contribute to this goal. It encourages the teaching team to share and build new based on their previous knowledge of what hinders learning and participation in their school. At the same time, it helps them to carry out a thorough and comprehensive analysis of the possibilities for improving the learning and participation of all their students. It should be noted that these tools should not be seen as just another initiative for schools, but as a systematic way of engaging in a school improvement plan, setting priorities for change, implementing innovations and evaluating processes. (Ainscow and Booth 2002a).

The Index was primarily developed for use in schools, so that all participants (including families, as will be seen) could review, rethink and explore their practices; and in this evaluation, recognize shortcomings and strengths that could lead to a process of institutional improvement, in terms of greater inclusion. Therefore, it is important to point out that the usefulness of the application of the Index was not restricted in its formulation to a rating of the level of inclusion of an educational center; its purpose was and is to set the school community thinking, based on a diagnosis, in order to move towards concrete proposals that would enable greater inclusion. It is structured on the identification of situations or characteristics that correspond to three areas or perspectives: cultures, practices and policies. Thus, these are the three axes it probes into and, consequently, it will be in relation to them that work should be done in order to make headway in the progressive growth of educational inclusion. The Index proposes to identify, on the one hand, how inclusive the school culture is, i.e., the values and perceptions incorporated in a given educational community, so that it should be a community that has room for the particularities and challenges presented by its members, and does so in a collaborative environment. It also explores school practices by focusing on the actions and behaviors that define the daily life of the school, in order to assess (and then eliminate) the obstacles that prevent the participation of all students in school life. Finally, it focuses on policies, to the extent that they can guide towards greater inclusion through the development of innovative projects that focus on learning for all. The Index proposes a real work process that includes five-stage planning for improvement. It is a tool for educational innovation that aims to admit and welcome change in the culture and values of each educational center, so that inclusive practices are adopted regardless of the identification of particular priorities. To this end, educational change today requires re-evaluating slow knowing, learning in context, and a type of leadership that can no longer be that of the few but of the many, who feel the awakening of personal commitment (Fullan, 2001).[2]

---

2 The Index proposes a five-stage process consisting of: (1) initiation of the process; (2) analysis of the educational center; (3) elaboration of the school improvement plan with an inclusive orientation; (4) implementation of the aspects that can be improved; and (5) evaluation of the Index process. In turn, it is conceptually structured on three interrelated dimensions considered equally important, whose selection is intended to focus on the necessary changes. Thus, the three dimensions of the Index are: Dimension A "Creating Inclusive CULTURES"; Dimension B "Formulating Inclusive POLICIES"; Dimension C "Developing Inclusive PRACTICES". Dimension A "Creating Inclusive Cultures" refers to the creation of a school community with inclusive values shared by all teachers, students, school board members and families in the community, to develop a welcoming and collaborative educational community, whose foundation is the valuing of each other, so that all students attain higher levels of achievement. Dimension B "Formulating Inclusive Policies" seeks to place inclusion at the core of innovation and of all policies, focused on improving participation and learning. Thus, in order to cater

This Index is taken in this work as an inspiration for the survey on the level of inclusion perceived in the system. Although it could not be said that this is a straightforward application of the same instrument (since it is done in a reduced form -only the form for teachers is taken, and the number of questions is reduced- in addition to being done for diagnostic purposes), its redesign and adaptation was carried out with the greatest possible adherence to the outline and content of the Index. The wording of the questions is very similar, but the reduction in the number of questions, together with the fact that its application was restricted to members of the General Inspection Directorate of the Directorate-General for Culture and Education (i.e., school inspectors, district inspectors and regional inspectors, excluding the remaining school members), and carried out at one and the same point in time, meant a significant modification with respect to the document that served as inspiration for the present work.

It is worth pointing out here, then, that the application of the Index presents some differences in this research with respect to that of the Ainscow and Booth team, mainly because in this case it was done with the objective of obtaining an internal view (from the officials of the education system itself in the strict sense, that is, without the participation, in the broad sense, of the community, which includes families and other members, and without involving teachers and school administrators) as an internal diagnosis, and not as the actual beginning of the process of change (although it may eventually serve this purpose). It is worth making it clear that a true and in-depth adaptation (which has consciously been avoided, limiting it strictly to what is unavoidable for its application) would entail a separate study in itself.

---

for diversity, support to institutions will increase, but this support will no longer be designed from the perspective of administrative structures, but with a view to the development of all students. Finally, Dimension C "Developing Inclusive Practices" focuses on school and extracurricular activities to ensure that they allow for the participation of all students and consider not only their school experiences, but also those outside the school environment.

In turn, for the design of the Inclusion Index, its authors structured each of the proposed Dimensions on two sections, focusing on the activities that are considered essential as a way to improve learning and participation. These are: In Dimension A "Creating Inclusive Cultures", the activities consist in building community and establishing inclusive values; Dimension B "Formulating Inclusive Policies" is about developing a school for all and organizing attention to diversity; and in Dimension C "Developing Inclusive Practices" the activities consist in instrumenting learning processes and mobilizing resources. These same dimensions and sections can then be used to design the school improvement plan. Going to the initial application of the index (stages 1 and 2 of the Index process and the improvement planning cycle), each section contemplates a variety of indicators, each of which is identified with a set of questions. In total, there are 45 indicators corresponding to a total of 511 questions.

5

DEVELOPMENT OF RESEARCH

5.1. THE EDUCATION SYSTEM OF THE PROVINCE OF BUENOS AIRES: ORGANIZATION

The surface area of the Province of Buenos Aires (slightly over 300,000 square kilometers), as well as its population size (approximately 18 million people) grant it a position of great relevance in Argentine reality; this is due to its geographical location (adjacent to Buenos Aires city, with access to both the Río de La Plata and the ocean, approximately in the very center of the country´s eastern border), as well as to the size of its labor force -the result of the work and economic activity of the province. It is home to approximately 40% of the overall population of Argentina, and to important production centers, which account for nearly 38% of the country´s GDP. Its population is quite unevenly distributed, a natural result of its large surface area and the characteristics of the various productive activities carried out (mainly agriculture and livestock rearing further into the province, manufacturing and/or commercial activities in the urban areas surrounding Buenos Aires city). While rural areas are sparsely populated, population becomes markedly concentrated as one moves nearer Buenos Aires city, where, apart from highly urbanized towns, there appear precarious housing settlements that lack basic services such as drinking water, a sewerage system and mains gas supply. The fact that a significant part of the population commute daily to Buenos Aires city has given rise to the denomination AMBA (Metropolitan Area of Buenos Aires, for its initials in Spanish), to refer to the area common to both jurisdictions.

As for the dynamics of its education system –with over 5 million students enrolled and 400 thousand employees on its payroll-, the Province of Buenos Aires has proved to be highly autonomous at the time of implementing education reforms, not only as a result of the aforementioned characteristics but also due to its traditions, resources and political forces, not to mention that it boasts the longest-standing education system; besides, the appointment of the minister (Director-General for Culture and Education) requires approval from the Legislature of the Province (Gorostiaga, Acedo and González, 2004). Its autarchy is specifically contemplated in the Constitution of the Province (art. 201). A collegiate body (in existence since the first constitution of the province in 1873), the General Council for Culture and Education (as it is named today) is presided over by the Director-General, who has the rank of minister. It is, therefore, a province that imbues its education system with characteristics that are specific to it, reflecting the considerable differences it presents not only in terms of population dispersion but also of the characteristics of said population, where there exists a wide socio-economic gap.

In terms of the structure of its legislation and within the federal scheme of the country's national organization, the province regulates its functioning with the autonomy allowed by the federalism of government, in line with the guidelines at the national level. This organization implies a complex network of relations and competences concerning the government and administration of the education system, depending on its spheres, which generates different types of relations, as explained by Caldo and Mariani (2020):

> As to what pertains to the governance and administration of the education system, the National Constitution lists a number of competences, some exclusive of the federal state, others, exclusive of the member states, some specifically prohibited, others that are common ground and subject to regulation by the federal state as well as by the member states. It is possible to recognize relationships of supra-subordination (federal supremacy over member states), inordination (involving the participation of member states in the shaping of the federal will) and coordination (involving the allocation of competences between federal state and member states). Said enumeration of competences denotes a specific type of relationship established between the two centers of power: coordination relationships, which are part of a complex network of relationships and

regulations deriving from the federal system and which should coexist in harmony; however, federal regulations and national policies are interwoven with regulations and policies of the province, making the relationship between central and local powers even more complex. (2020, p.1)

The main regulatory bodies are Provincial Education Law 13688 (referred to in the introduction of the topic) and the Teachers' Statute (Law 10579, and amendments), which focuses on the organization of the teaching activity itself. For its part, in its Constitution, the Province of Buenos Aires recognizes culture and education as fundamental human rights, assumes education as a non-delegable responsibility of the Province (art. 198), admits that education is aimed at respecting human rights and fundamental freedoms in the principles of Christian morality and freedom of conscience (art. 199), and establishes that the education service is also provided through private or public non-state subjects, all of which make up the provincial education system under state control (art. 200).

The organization of legislation, in particular the constitutional provisions concerning education, in line with freedom, equality and the right to non-discrimination, is testimony to the conceptual evolution throughout the world -at least in the western world- of the right to education. After the Second World War (with the creation of the United Nations Organization in 1945 and a new global dynamic), this began to take shape as a true human right, recognized in the most important documents (Declarations, Conventions, Treaties) of international law: the 1948 Universal Declaration of Human Rights recognizes the right to free elementary education for the purpose of the full development of the personality and the preferential right of parents to choose the education of their children (art. 26); the International Covenant on Economic, Social and Cultural Rights of 1966 postulates the right of everyone to education (art. 13); the International Covenant on Civil and Political Rights of the same year (1966) enshrines freedom of thought and of choice of education (art. 18); the 1989 Convention on the Rights of the Child provides, in particular, for the right to free education (Art. 23) and, in the case of the "disabled child", the right to enjoy a full life in conditions of self-sufficiency and with active participation in the community (Art. 23); finally, the Convention on the Rights of Persons with Disabilities of 2006 postulates in plain terms the right to inclusive education (art. 24). Consequently, -and as mentioned above- this is what has been called the transnational dimension of Law and Justice (Cappelletti, 1994), which implies not only the recognition of "equal and inalienable rights of all members of the human family" (UN Charter, 1945) but also the subordination of each signatory country to a common legal order, a subordination that goes beyond the obligations between countries, to imply direct obligations towards their citizens. On the possibility of taking action for the particular recognition of these rights, see the work of Cappelletti and Garth (1996). It is interesting that, just as Ainscow and Booth propose three dimensions related to educational inclusion, the great Italian jurist, dedicated to the study of comparative law, also proposes three dimensions of comparative justice: the constitutional dimension -linked to mechanisms for the protection of fundamental rights that guarantee human freedom and dignity-, the social dimension of justice -focused on access to justice as a means of guaranteeing citizens' equity- and the transnational dimension of justice -inherent to the process of globalization and integration between countries (see Mac Gregor, 2009).

This global phenomenon led, in the specific case of inclusive education, to a commitment to public international law on the part of Argentina (as a state signatory to the aforementioned documents) to adopt all appropriate measures -legislative, administrative and others- to give effect to the rights of persons with disabilities. This includes modifying and repealing discriminatory laws, regulations and practices, as well as taking into consideration in all policies and programs the promotion of the rights of persons with disabilities and taking all measures to ensure that no organization discriminates on the basis of disability (General Obligations, art. 4, Convention on the Rights of Persons with Disabilities). The Convention also states the obligation to ensure at all levels an inclusive education system that enables the full development of human potential and reinforces respect for human freedom and diversity, makes possible the full development of the personality, talents and creativity of persons with disabilities, and enables their effective participation in a free society (Art. 24). In accordance with the above, the National Constitution of Argentina, as well as the Constitution of the Province of Buenos Aires recognize the right to teach and learn (art. 14 National Constitution & art. 35 BA Province Constitution), the principle of equality before the law (art. 16 National Constitution & art. 11 BA Province Constitution), and the principle of reserve, whereby no one can be deprived of that which the law does not expressly prohibit (art. 19 National Constitution & art. 25 BA Province Constitution). "The National Constitution, the laws passed in consequence thereof and the treaties signed with foreign powers being the supreme law of the Nation, the authorities of each province are obliged to conform to it" (art. 31 National Constitution), as universal declarations and human rights conventions enjoy constitutional status (Section 74, subsection 22, paragraph 2 of the National Constitution and Law 27066).

In order to honor Argentina's commitment before its own citizens to adapt its regulations for their acknowledgement and effective implementation, in 2016, the Federal Education Council issued Resolution 311/2016, which takes as its crux the Convention on the Rights of Persons with Disabilities. Consequently, it incorporates into the Argentinean education system a new paradigm on disability. At the same time, it urges the adaptation of local education systems to "promote the necessary conditions for school inclusion within the Argentinean education system for the accompaniment of students with disabilities as they go through school" (art. 1). Along the same lines of advancement of this education reform, and as a facilitator for its compliance throughout the territory, the Ministry of Education and Sports of the Nation issued an "Orientation Guide for the implementation of Resolution 311 of the Federal Council of Education of Dec. 15, 2016" (approved by Resolution 2509/17), followed by the recognition of national validity of certificates (Resolution 2945/17).

Against this backdrop, the Province of Buenos Aires followed suit and, through its Director-General for Culture and Education, issued the regulations for its local implementation, initially through Resolution 1664/2017. The modifications introduced by this Resolution are profound, among them not only the incorporation of inclusive contents in the curriculum and the institutional school project, but also the freedom of choice of modality for students and their families, the elimination of the previous mandatory double enrollment in special and mainstream schools, training of teachers in the topic of inclusion, new rules for certification and promotion, as well as a new dynamic of interaction and cooperation between levels and modality, among others. The resolution repeals the prior regulation and endorses the document "Inclusive Education in the Province of Buenos Aires for children, adolescents, youths and young adults with disabilities ", which includes the following sections: "Inclusive Education in the Province of Buenos Aires", "The inclusion of children with disabilities at Initial Level"; "The inclusion of students with disabilities at Primary School Level", "The inclusion of students with disabilities at Secondary School Level" and "Inclusive Education Trajectories in the Special Educational modality". Subsequently, the Director-General for Culture and Education of the Province of Buenos Aires issued resolution 4891/18 (Official Bulletin number 28423 of the BA Province of December 18, 2018) which sets the guidelines for the accreditation /certification in Secondary Education, Technical Vocational Education, Artistic Education and Adult Education on equal terms for students with disabilities. Finally, in this provincial jurisdiction, the document "Inclusive and quality education, a right for all" was issued; it is a collaborative work created together with a network of civil society organizations, written in clear language, which highlights the central aspects that make for the effective school inclusion in the Province of Buenos Aires education system of students with disabilities (Resolution 6257/2019 RESFC 6257- Directorate-General for Culture and Education -19); in addition, it includes in the design of the new primary school curriculum a module on inclusive education. On the evolution of regulations concerning inclusive education in the Province of Buenos Aires, see Saccon (2018), which, though prior to the resolutions on certification and the general document issued for the BA province, clearly sets forth the general and particular principles of inclusive education, contrasts them with local reality and the difficulties for their implementation, highlights the remarkable progress brought about by the issuing of Resolution 1664/2017 for the jurisdiction, and points out the differences between regulatory and cultural progress, as well as the scenario of resistance on the part of teachers and institutions.

In short, the above is proof that, for the actual and practical implementation of inclusion in school life -as for any educational reform, innovation or change- a true and extensive collaborative and participatory process will be required on the part of teachers and members of the school community. This is a reform of the type aimed to democratize school management (Gorostiaga: 2007), since, although not implying greater freedom and/or autonomy for teachers, it does contemplate greater -it might now be called decisive- participation of families in making decisions about the schooling of their children with disabilities. In these terms, it would be a model of decentralization of school management based on community control. This is so since, though in a way revitalizing Institutional Education Projects, the reform does so in order to impose inclusive contents; it focuses on increasing the involvement of new participants, identified as the parents of students with disabilities, and the team of professionals involved in their care, all of whom it places in a position of relevance and from a legal perspective of right. Thus, as mentioned above, reforms owe -to a large extent- their success or failure not only to institutional solutions, but also to variables outside the school environment involving families. In this sense, the "choice and exit" approach developed by Albert Hirschman in the 1970s furnishes the world of education with very interesting clues for the understanding of the counterweight exercised by certain interest groups with regard to education policies, especially in Latin America (Di John, 2007). Thus, as with any reform, its implementation will depend on a variety of participants, and it is the dynamics of cooperation and resistance that will make inclusion a reality. Ainscow and Booth's Index for Inclusion, which -with the appropriate adaptations- sets the general direction of our survey, is aimed precisely at detecting these resistances, obstacles and tensions.

5.2. THE EDUCATION SYSTEM OF THE PROVINCE OF BUENOS AIRES: CHARACTERISTICS

The most recent official report that provides the main data on the education system of the province is condensed in the report "2019. El estado de la escuela" (2019. The State of Schools), published by the Dirección General de Cultura y Educación de la Provincia de Buenos Aires (Directorate-General for Education and Culture of the Province of Buenos Aires) in December 2019. This report presents a general diagnosis of the situation of education in the BA province, based on data obtained from the national standardized APRENDER assessments of the Secretariat of Educational Evaluation of the Ministry of Education of Argentina, the 2010 National Census and the Encuesta Permanente de Hogares- EPH (Permanent Household Surveys) of the Instituto Nacional de Estadística y Censos - INDEC (National Statistics and Census Institute) and the Relevamiento Anual- RA (Annual Surveys) of the Dirección de Información y Estadística (Statistics and Information Directorate).

For the purposes of this section, which sets out to describe the specific and current reality of the education system of the province, the above-mentioned report will be closely adhered to, because it is the most recent -and highly relevant- publication, not to mention the fact that it indicates its sources. The following is a transcription of the main data that helps to describe this education system; unless otherwise indicated, the information refers to the year 2019:

- The BA province education system comprises 19,387 schools, annexes and education extensions. Of these, 13,408 are provincial; 5,500 are privately managed; 429 are under the aegis of municipal authorities, and 50 are under the administration of the nation or of other agencies. The school population is in excess of 5 million students.
- 84.6% of all enrollees attend pre-school, primary and secondary school.
- The disaggregation of standard enrollment by education level is the following: 17.5% pre-school education; 40% primary school education; 36.4% secondary school education and 6.1% higher education.
- 15.4% of total enrollment corresponds to the eight modalities of education offered consecutively or complementarily to regular education (Technical Vocational Education; Special Education; Permanent Education for Youth, Adults, Older Adults and Vocational Training; Artistic Education, Physical Education, Community Psychology and Social Pedagogy; Intercultural Education and Environmental Education).

- Disaggregation by modality is as follows: 58.4% Youth and Adult Education, 19% Physical Education, 11.8% Special Education, 6.9% Artistic Education and 4% Psychology (note that other modalities include transversal contents incorporated into the levels).
- The administration of educational establishments may correspond, according to the case, to an entity under the aegis of the General Directorate of Culture and Education (Ministry of Education of the Province) for provincial establishments, to their owners and municipalities for private and/or municipal state-run establishments, or to other provincial ministries.
- In terms of overall population, the age of 4.3 million inhabitants of the province ranges from 4 to 17, still at the stage of mandatory education. 96.7% of them attend school.
- Enrollment in 2018 reached 5.1 million, 40% of the country total.
- Disaggregation of enrollment in the BA province is as follows: 67.4% province-dependent schools, 30.5% private schools, 1.7% municipal schools and 0.4% schools administered by the national state or other agencies.
- In the period 2017-2018, total enrollment grew by 1.3%: this occurred in schools run by the province; private enrollment, in turn, fell. In the same period, 243 schools opened, which meant a 1.3% increase.
- Enrollment has grown by 148% in the last 5 years.
- The system comprises 200,000 sections or courses, 70% of which are state establishment at the provincial level; 27.8% are private institutions; and 2.2% are administered by municipal and national entities or other bodies. Mainstream education comprises 169,540 sections or courses; modalities, 30,547.
- In terms of pupil/teacher ratio (pupils per section), although the overall figures show a lower ratio in state-run schools than in private schools (state pre-school 24.5 pupils per section compared to 25 in private schools; state primary 24.3 compared to 29.1 in private schools, 24 pupils in state secondary school level compared to 28.9 in private schools), these figures admit various interpretations (at primary school level, presumably due to the distortion caused by

low level of enrollment in rural schools, and at secondary school level, due to the number of students dropping out of school, which is higher in state schools).

- The effective Promotion Rate at primary school level is slightly lower in the state sector than in the private sector (95.5% vs. 96.3%), while at secondary school level the gap is much wider (91.7% in the private sector vs. 82.4% in the state sector). The repetition rate (students failing to be promoted) shows the same phenomenon of inequity (private primary schools 0.8% versus 4.8% in state primary schools; private secondary schools 4.8% vs. 12.9% in state secondary schools).

- The Annual Dropout Rate was 2.9% in state schools vs. 3.8 % in the private sector. The exception occurred in primary state school, where no students dropped out (-0.5%); rather students coming from the private sector or other jurisdictions were welcomed into state schools.

- The Over-Age Rate of students in secondary school level is 4 times that in primary school level (29% vs. 7.3%), a more frequent phenomenon in state-run schools.

- In 2019, the indicators of internal efficiency of the secondary school level in the state sector showed improvement, as well as a narrowing of the gap with the results of its private counterparts; in the primary school level, however, the indicators of state schools showed virtually no variations.

- In compliance with requirements, the APRENDER (LEARNING) national standardized evaluation was carried out in the BA province in 2016, 2017 and 2018. The students of the final year of the primary and secondary school cycles were evaluated; the results in language were better than in mathematics, though in general terms, neither were satisfactory. There appeared to be a year-on-year trend towards improvement in the results in language.

- The education system is organized in 5 regions (which group districts) in order to administrate, accompany and supervise education activity in the 135 districts of the BA province.

- The structure of the system has undergone major transformations in the last 15 years, as a result not only of the need to organize the availability of education but also of the effect of new regulatory frameworks (national and provincial education laws). The province, through its Directorate-General for Education and Culture (law 13688 of the BA province), is responsible for providing, guaranteeing and supervising inclusive, permanent and quality education for all its inhabitants from age 4 to the end of secondary school. This is the mandatory cycle of school education.
- The coverage of primary education (of mandatory and free-of-charge nature guaranteed by law, as well as secondary education) is practically universal and is organized in a 6-year pedagogical unit, with a new curricular design dating from 2017 (Resolution No. 1482/DGC&E -Directorate-General for Culture and Education- of 2017). Secondary education is also organized in a minimum of 6 years (with a Basic or General Cycle common to all orientations followed by an Oriented Cycle).
- Students with a disability account for 1.7% of the total 92,632 students. Half of them attend special schools; the remaining half, mainstream schools.

In the preceding transcription of data, the following has been intentionally omitted: information on enrollment, graduation (and corresponding norms and regulations, among them laws on higher education and technical-vocational education) referring to non-mandatory education levels, including vocational (teacher) training cycles. The reason for this omission is that this is not a priori of particular interest for the purposes of the present work. The full, precise and detailed explanation of the legal-bureaucratic organization of the complete education system in the Province of Buenos Aires, the provision of the educational service and its forms, as well as the characteristics of all educational modalities and teacher-training institutions would render this research inadequately and unnecessarily lengthy. The aim of both this and the preceding section has been to go over the legal organization of the system with reference to the fundamental right (the right to inclusive education) and present data on education management within it. Finally, and although they are outside the strictly academic sphere -since they are essays or publications on current political affairs- mention must be made of the works of Sánchez Zinny (2020), Narodowski (2018) and Rovner and Monjeau (2017); the first two held the positions of Ministers in the Province of Buenos Aires and in the Autonomous City of Buenos Aires, respectively. These works are useful to complete the picture of the national and provincial reality and dynamics of education of the Province of Buenos Aires, and the tensions existing within it.

5.3. METHODOLOGY: DESCRIPTIVE STUDY OF THE QUANTITATIVE TYPE

When the subject was introduced, the reason or interest of this exploratory research was stated; it was also pointed out that it was to be a descriptive and quantitative study, as it sought to measure variables and play them off against each other; there existed no prior hypothesis about their concordance. The present work consists, then, in measuring the perceived level of inclusion; the variables for measuring are derived from the chosen theoretical framework: on the one hand, the measurement of three levels of inclusion and the dimensions proposed by Ainscow and Booth in the elaboration of their Index Code; on the other hand, following Sally Tomlinson's Sociology of Special Education, the characteristics of the respondents and their position (roles, interests) within the education system. The focal interest is to diagnose, from the point of view of the body of inspectors, what is the level of inclusion in the education system of the BA province, as well as its size, obtain a scale score of perception of inclusion of each dimension and for the overall education system of the BA province, correlate perception with some personal data of respondents (training, level or modality, age, length of service, etc.) and finally, to reflect upon the application of this diagnosis for the design and implementation of policies and plans aiming at an improved level of inclusion.

A survey was therefore deemed the adequate methodological strategy in this case, as it is a quantitative research based on verbal statements of a specific population (members of the body of inspectors) carried out to ascertain opinion on a specific topic, in this case, the level of inclusion of the education system of the BA province (Aravena, Kimelman, Micheli, Torrealba and Zúñiga, 2006). This is a structured, standardized and self-administered questionnaire, including close-ended questions, that was administered twice (to different people) to elicit the opinion of the universe of the population involved. The survey was administered to all those who attended two meetings at provincial level (no previous selection was made, so there was no prior sampling procedure); naturally, attendees are not the total population of existing inspectors. It should be noted that the invitation to the two meetings, held in the city of La Plata, was issued to the entire body of inspectors (school, district and regional inspectors). Some of the expenses to be incurred (such as transportation) were to be covered by the organizers; however, it cannot be disregarded that the attendance of some and the absence of others may have been dictated by the distances involved, the additional costs that a trip may entail (accommodation for the night among others), the personal circumstances of each inspector faced with an, in some cases, long journey and even the specific interest or incentive of each inspector. Of the total number of inspectors (1,734), the response rate was slightly below one-fifth (18.56%), as the opinions of 322 persons were obtained. This is certainly a limitation of this research, since the data obtained do not make it possible to ascertain how representative the set of respondents is of the total population. Although for the subsequent analysis of the data it would have been interesting to have information on the educational district each supervisor belonged to (identifying district, region) and thus detect, on the one hand, differences in the perceived levels of inclusion according to locality, and, on the other hand, possible causes of absence due to distance, the request for this information was intentionally not included in the preliminary or personal data questionnaire; the reason was that it was understood that adding a request for specification of region or jurisdiction to the information already required (position, level or modality, length of service and sex) would render identification of each one of them extremely simple; thus, the survey would cease to be anonymous; this might, in fact, curtail the freedom and compromise the candor of responses, which was the overriding priority in this work.

1. The survey meets the requirements of reliability and internal validity: standardized answers, clearly formulated questions and

indicators valid to measure the proposed concepts. Let it be borne in mind, on the other hand, that the Index employed as the basis for this survey has been validated by research carried out in a number of different countries, albeit not at systemic level but at the level of individual or groups of educational institutions. Though adapted to a much more general sample - such as that of the present work - it is, then, a measurement tool that enjoys credibility and reliability in the academia; its application to an education system as a whole is precisely the objective of this study. With regard to survey design and how it has been adapted, the following should be highlighted: The survey is preceded by a preliminary questionnaire on the respondent's personal information. Thus, the questionnaire designed consists of a First Section containing the 13-question "Personal Data Questionnaire", followed by the "Survey Questionnaire".

2. Unlike the original Index for Inclusion, designed not only as a measurement tool but primarily as a trigger for a process of institutional change and, therefore, meant to be responded to at different times by different participants, the present tool has a cross-section or transversal design, which allows information to be collected at the same point in time.

3. It considers the structure of the Index Code in terms of the three dimensions to be analyzed (Cultures, Policies and Practices), their indicators and the corresponding questions for each of them. The "Survey Questionnaire" is organized in three sections or general variables, related to the dimensions of the Index. The First Dimension, "Cultures", proposes 8 intermediate variables (partial aspects for each dimension), each including 4 questions or items, i.e. 4 empirical variables, the directly observable aspects. The Second Dimension, "Policies", includes 9 intermediate variables with 4 indicators for each of them, and the Third Dimension, "Practices", proposes 9 variables with 4 indicators each.

4. The operationalization of the variables leads from general variables (the three dimensions mentioned above) to intermediate variables or questions, which constitute the partial aspects for each dimension. 8/9 intermediate variables have been selected

from among those proposed in the original Index for each general variable, which makes a total of 26 intermediate variables. In turn, each intermediate variable is operationalized into indicators or empirical variables, the directly observable aspects: the items of our survey. There are 4 items or empirical variables (identified as a-b-c-d) for a total of 26 intermediate variables.

5. The Likert scale was used as a measurement rule for each of the items; four possible mutually exclusive responses were offered (ordinal variables from highest to lowest). Although they correspond to the options proposed by Ainscow and Booth, their wording is different, since in the Index for Inclusion the possible responses consisted in affirming or denying the existence of practices considered inclusive in the respondent´s school (consequently, the response options were graded as follows:" "fully agree/ agree/ disagree/ need more information"). In the present case, for each indicator or item, four possible mutually exclusive response options are also offered, ranked from highest to lowest, presented in the form of columns; but this being an application to an education system and not to any school in particular, the response options offered are: "Yes, in most schools", "Yes, in some schools", "In almost no schools" and "I lack information". When this survey was adapted, the options and the scheme were conceptually respected, extending it to a larger number of schools, so that the perception was not restricted to one school but comprised all schools under the respondent's supervision. This gradation measures the level of inclusion from high to low. The option 'Yes, in few schools' was not included for two reasons: (i) to avoid an uneven number of possible answers, which usually encourages adopting the intermediate position, consequently making answers of neutral value (zero-sum); and (ii) because the intention was to force a decision in the general view of that inspector regarding the schools under their supervision.

6. Each column corresponds to a different level of perceived inclusiveness, from highest to lowest. The selection of these options will result for each item in a rating as "very inclusive", "relatively inclusive", "not very inclusive", and "no information". Although the fourth option might seem to be useless in relation to the values

for each category (according to the Lickert scale), it is found in the original Index; furthermore, it was decided to keep it because of its usefulness for the detection of dimensions and items for which no opinion on the level of inclusion can be obtained, but which indicate the need to delve more deeply into this aspect of inclusion, be it the information available to the agents involved or reinforcement of its implementation, as the case may be. If the members of the supervisory team express a majority (high frequency level) of "lack of knowledge" about one of the items, this would indicate that this variable is important for the purpose of emphasizing the need for public policy makers to go into it in greater depth. Another possible interpretation could also be that, depending on the issue on which the respondent claims not to have information, this response could also show reluctance on their part to give their opinion. Since this fourth column does not measure perceived level of inclusion, but rather non-response (due to lack of information or reluctance), for the purpose of processing and presenting data on levels of inclusion, only the average frequency of the three previous options will be considered ('Yes, in most schools', 'Yes, in some schools', 'In almost no schools'), corresponding to the three proposed levels: very inclusive, relatively inclusive, not very inclusive.

7. Processing the survey data consists in measuring the frequency of each response, i.e. the number of cases for each category (corresponding to each column in the design). The measurement utilized establishes intra- and inter-variable relationships. The variable(s) with the highest frequency of response in column 3 (equivalent to "not very inclusive"), will point to those aspects where a low level of inclusion is identified and, therefore, where the given situation should be reviewed and strategies thought out to achieve a higher level of inclusion. On the other hand, higher level of frequency in the fourth column ("I lack information") might indicate the need to increase intra-system communication, so that supervisory members have, in future, data that will enable them to opt between options 1 to 3 for that specific item.

8. It should be made clear that the questionnaire used was Index Questionnaire 1, i.e. the main questionnaire, and not

those especially adapted for students, families or the school (Index Questionnaires 2 and 3). In order to make possible their simultaneous application in short meetings, the number of questions for each indicator was reduced and the breaking down of each indicator into the two practices proposed for each of the three dimensions was omitted. In doing so, we reduced a questionnaire of 511 questions to a survey of 26 questions or intermediate variables.

As for the sampling proper, it was carried out on two occasions, always in the form of a self-administered survey and with the presence of the administrator. It was done with the participation and introduction of the Director of General Inspection (Adriana Frega) and the Director of Special Education (initially Daniel Del Torto, later followed in the position by Juan Pablo Eviner), to all attendees of the meeting of the Directorate for General Inspection on 29 May 2018, and the provincial symposium on Inclusive Education held in the city of La Plata on June 29, 2018, both organized by the Directorate-General for Education and Culture. Previously, invitations to both meetings were extended by these Directorates to all inspectors of all modalities, levels and districts of the province; all those who actually attended the meetings were asked to complete the survey.

9. The sample results may have been influenced by the vicinity or distance of the district under supervision and the place where the survey was taken. Note, in this respect, that this is evidenced by the very low level of participation of regional chief inspectors; out of a total of 25 educational regions (each with two chiefs, one for each type of administration) only 2 participants reported they occupied this position. This circumstance renders the findings regarding the perception of Regional Chief Inspectors hardly representative.

10. On both occasions, the time limit to complete the survey was one hour, so in order to allow sufficient time for reading and answering it, the index had to be adapted and reduced in terms of number of questions and indicators. Other references to issues unrelated to the organization of the Province of Buenos Aires education system were deleted, and/or others were included, such as the role of parents' organizations.

The questionnaire was in paper format, inspectors had no previous contact with the survey (on the first date it was conducted). On the second one, those who had participated and completed it in the previous meeting were instructed not to answer it. The number of inspectors who indicated that they had participated in the previous meeting and did not accept the printed form, basically tallied with the previous number of participants; however, there is no way to assert this was absolutely accurate; there could have been isolated cases, although numerically negligible, of either absence or duplication of responses, that went undetected.

Finally, it seems important to point out that it was repeatedly indicated, both at the moment of handing out the questionnaire and while it was being answered, that there were no right or wrong answers, that the information they provided would not have any impact whatsoever on any type of evaluation (in terms of scoring, marking or grading) of any kind regarding supervisory or teaching work, nor of the schools´ performance, but that the objective was to get information concerning their own perception of the reality of the schools under their supervision. Therefore, the surveys were anonymous. It was also stated that the information would be used in the present research (this information was incorporated as an explanatory note at the beginning of the form).

The full text of the printed form is included in the corresponding Annex. Albeit created by the research team, it was checked with the participation of officials with a technical profile. The survey was officially endorsed by the Directorate-General for Culture and Education of the Province of Buenos Aires, as evinced by the corresponding logo printed at the top of each page of the form. As pointed out when the relevance of the questionnaire was indicated, and in line with the tenets of action research, the responses were an extremely important source of information for detecting impediments and designing plans and programs to consolidate greater effective educational inclusion in all the districts of the Province of Buenos Aires. Though not an evaluation in terms of grading, it was a diagnostic evaluation, and during the administration of the then Director-General, Sánchez Zinny, this became standard practice (see Sánchez Zinny, 2020, p. 62). In a way, its objective was to ensure that educational innovation or change does not arise from a context different from the one in which it will be applied (Viñao, 2002), but that it draws on it in terms of design and subsequent success. Ultimately, it is meant to strengthen ties and attain a type of communication between researchers and political decision-makers that is not only more effective for the good of the education system, but that includes those who, outside this binary classification, are members of the educational community and play a role that cannot be obviated.

5.4. ADAPTING THE INDEX FOR INCLUSION TO THE STUDY: IMPLEMENTATION OF THE SURVEY THROUGH THE BODY OF INSPECTORS

As explained in the description of the education system in the Province of Buenos Aires, it comprises a large area, divided into 25 educational regions to administer, support and supervise educational activity in the 135 municipalities of the province. This means that school organization is ultimately - and to a very large extent - managed by the Supervision, in particular because of the significant distances between educational regions. At the time of the survey, the overall number of inspectors was 1,734 taking into account both state and private schools. Of these, 132 were district chief inspectors, 43 regional chief inspectors and the others were school inspectors.

The figure of the inspector, their role and functions, as well as the supervision systems, are many-sided, as pointed out in the theoretical framework. However, even with the limitations described therein, inspectors play a central role in the implementation of plans, programs or reforms, since it is through them that the replication of an action plan, program or reform can be accomplished simultaneously throughout the territory. This is also due to the highly vertical nature of the system, a phenomenon possibly finding its causes not only in the idiosyncrasy of teachers but also in the particular provisions of their statute, which contemplates school organization on the basis of a rigid system (in terms of its functions, roles and remuneration), and formal hierarchical communication channels and assignment of responsibilities.

The Teachers' Statute (Provincial Law 10579 and amendments) devotes Chapter IV to the career structure ("Escalafón", as per the term in Spanish), which contemplates twenty positions ordered from the top down. The scale begins with "Positions in technical-pedagogical and organic-administrative management bodies" at the top (the highest being the Director de Repartición docente -Director of Teaching Departments-, followed by the deputy director) and, within this category, after the teaching advisors, are the members of the inspection team. This group of positions (also internally arranged hierarchically) corresponds to those considered civil servants, or those working at the level of the central organization. Inspectors are on the bottom rungs in this group, as they are the link between the Ministry and the schools. In descending hierarchical line, is the second category of Cargos en Servicios Educativos u Organismos de Apoyo Técnico, de Perfeccionamiento e Investigación-Positions in Education Services or Technical Support, Improvement and Research Bodies-, i.e. those who are part of specific education establishments where they discharge their duties. These are primary and secondary school principals, vice-principals, heads of interdisciplinary teams, first, second and third category principals, regular teachers, special teachers, school prefects, etc. In this structure, then, topmost is the ministry official who heads the political-pedagogical direction (director of the education level, director of modality, and/or director of supervision, all of them at the provincial level), down through to the school technical-pedagogical support staff, such as the school librarian (at the bottom of the list), including chief inspectors, chief secretaries, disciplinary teams, school principals, etc. The Teachers' Statute also regulates many other aspects of school life, which shape the profile of this profession and help characterize it: issues such as the definition of the organic-functional payroll (the so-called "POFs" -plantas orgánico-funcionales- of each school), the work of the rating boards (which are involved in the assessment of the order of candidates´ merit for filling vacant positions, entry into the teaching profession, promotions, among others), the annual assessment and rating of teachers by their immediate superior - who keeps their file (Arts. 127, 128), the behaviors considered breaches of discipline or disciplinary offences (Chapter XXII), their classification and sanctions, and the Disciplinary Boards that intervene in the eventual fact-finding procedures, make up the dynamics of this education system.

As can be seen, this is a particular structure of governance and administration with differentiated levels and relationships: a central level of governance conformed by the Directorate-General for Education and Culture and an intermediate level corresponding to the inspectorate, with different instances of district and regional heads which, although operating in the territory, respond and report hierarchically to the Directorate-General for Education and Culture. Thus, the education system in the BA province has three levels of management: a macro or central level, a middle level of regional and district heads, and schools at the micro level (Caldo and Mariani, 2020). The current supervisory system is organized around single regional and district heads, divided according to whether they supervise state-run or privately-run institutions, in such a way that school inspectors no longer respond or report to their branch or modality (as was the case before 2005), but rather to the same district head supervisor, who, in turn, reports to the regional head supervisor. This makes territorial education management more integrated, as heads are responsible for all teaching modalities. The configuration of the work and role of the supervisor coincided in time with the creation of the education system of the Province of Buenos Aires, although over time, the growing volume of norms and regulations has expanded the role of supervisors: from basic supervision of educational activity in the different areas of the territory to functions inside and outside the school, fashioned after a pedagogically based dual teaching model (monitoring, examining and simultaneously prescribing correct practices). The fact that access to positions is through professional competition differentiates inspectors from the political class: they progressively set themselves up as differentiated figures that function as links between political power and the education system (Ponce de León and Longobucco, 2008). The Ministry or Directorate-General for Education and Culture contemplates an organizational chart that defines its structure and assigns specific roles and functions to its officials. This is in addition to the provisions of the Teachers´ Statute regarding all those who make up the education system of the province (and have teaching positions) and the provisions of the provincial Education Act. In the case of the Directorate for General Inspection (whose director is, jointly with others, at the top of the aforementioned scale of the statute), according to resolution RESFC-2018-1107-GDEBA-DGC&E (2018a), it is responsible for a considerable number of various functions. Simultaneously, the Regional Heads must also fulfil a multiplicity of tasks.

It should be noted that with the change of government at the end of 2019 and shortly after a new Director-General for Culture and Education took office, the Ministry's organization chart was modified to include a significant expansion of its structure -resolution RESOC-2020-33-DGC&E-. However, as regards the roles, functions and tasks of the Directorate of Supervision or General Inspection, the modifications are of little relevance, so their detailed specification has been omitted -the characterization and profile of supervisors and inspectors remains the same-. In addition, it should be noted that the sample for this research was obtained in 2018, i.e. under the structure that provided for the roles, functions and tasks specified above.

In short, inspectors are considered to be the eyes and ears of the central authority in the actual field, provide support to teachers and principals as they discharge their duties and contribute to the solution of any issues that may arise. As the people with maximum responsibility for management in each part of the province, inspectors know the schools of their level and modality, the realities of their district, and are a very important source of information for decision-making at the ministerial level.

> The traditional role of supervisors has been to transmit and enforce the legal norms of the education system issued at the central level; however, they have little decision-making capacity, except when implicitly delegated by central authorities. Supervisors influence the work of schools by interpreting, "translating" and communicating norms, which became an important function in the context of an education policy expressed through ministerial resolutions. (Gorostiaga, Acedo and González, 2004, p. 9).

In addition to the above, another central fact is that most inspectors are former teachers who have climbed up the professional ladder (remember the career structure), so that, in addition to being in contact with the schools in their district, level and modality as a natural part of their supervisory work, due to their previous work, they are well acquainted with the internal, daily and local dynamics; they are "children of the system". They have been in it for years; they have experienced it; they know its internal dynamics and the particulars of school life. At the same time, they belong to -and possibly identify with- a specific sector (level, branch, modality, type of education), all of which may influence their positioning and their perception of school reality and its level of inclusion. They know, in Viñao's terms, the black box of school reality, the rituals of school life and of environmental factors, graduation, ways of assessment, the specific cultures of each school, of each education level and of each of the groups of agents involved in the day-to-day life of teaching institutions, as well as more specific subcultures (2002). See the aforementioned work by Caldo and Mariani (2020) regarding the characterization of the supervisor´s role, its various facets, the organization of the Directorate for General Inspection, the double-reporting functional structure (pedagogical and political) traversed by its own tensions (resulting from a task that stands between administrative and pedagogical knowledge, and from being a means to transmit education policies from the central level of government to schools), the progressive transformation of its functions and roles, as well as its political affiliation.

For all of the above, it can be considered that the team of supervisors constitutes a valuable primary source of information, which justifies their intervention at the moment of application of the instrument inspired by Ainscow and Booth's Index for Inclusion. This does not entail denial of the fact that inspectors often have, over many years, forged friendships and relationships -commitments even- with principals in their district. Not only that; they have some degree of responsibility (as they are in charge of supervision) for the results and implementation of inclusion policies in schools, i.e. because of their position, their responses are likely to lose a certain degree of naivety and be biased in that they might tend to 'defend' the system and its current situation and, consequently, attribute to it more inclusive characteristics than other members of the education system would. Notwithstanding this, their training, affinities and personal characteristics -for the categorization of which a preliminary questionnaire has been included- will also guide the detection of stands, biases and interests, from the perspective of Sally Tomlinson's Sociology of Special Education, the theoretical framework of this work.

5.5. PROCESSING OF DATA OBTAINED (TOOLS)

As previously indicated, the survey was taken as a print questionnaire -in writing, paper format-, using the single form appended in the Annex. Subsequently, for data processing, a Google Form was generated that replicated the questions in the survey. The characteristics of the Google Form were:

- Though at the time of the encounter, inspectors were asked to complete all the questions, some participants failed to answer some points. In view of that, the Google form was designed not making any answer mandatory; this way, failure to answer one question did not prevent respondents from continuing to answer the following points.
- Scoring of questions was omitted, thus making automatic evaluation possible.
- The survey was designed as a multiple-choice questionnaire with a linear scale and a grid of options.
- All the answers were of the multiple-choice type.
- More options had to be foreseen (as this was the processing tool) in case false or invalid answers were found, be it because they had been omitted or because more than one option had been selected (please remember that options were mutually exclusive).
- The columns correlate with the 4 columns provided in the paper questionnaire (1: "Yes, in most schools". 2: "Yes, in some schools." 3: "In almost no schools." 4: "I lack information.").
- Option 5 was employed when the participant failed to provide an answer in the questionnaire (blank), and option 6 was ticked when the answer was unclear or when more than one answer was provided. In the total number of surveys, the frequency of occurrence of these responses (5 and 6 in the Google Form) was negligible and, therefore, of marginal value.
- For the analysis of data in particular, Microsoft Power BI was used; all the data from the Google Form was exported to that platform,

which made it possible to cross-reference information and apply filters for the three dimensions, mainly related to the preliminary questionnaire -personal data-, and to present the results in different types of graphs. At the time of processing the information, and in order to make the presentation and results easier to read and understand, data was organized as follows:

- Items with omitted (blank) or more than one answer from the same participant (as already mentioned, both occurrences with marginal incidence), were assigned response values 4.1 and 4.2 respectively, and were therefore, included in response 4 of the survey, which corresponds to "I lack information", since the values are expressed as whole numbers, but allowing for disaggregation if necessary. Although in these cases there was no explicit acknowledgement on the part of the respondent of a lack of information (as they did not choose the given option as a response), the fact of not choosing any of the given options or having chosen two self-excluding options can be considered a non-response. It should be recalled that, given the functional role of inspectors in the education system, some resistance was to be expected to admitting lack of information, especially on the part of school and district inspectors (not so much on the part of regional inspectors -with minimal participation-, and whose relationship with each school is not so much of a day-to-day nature).

- Results have been averaged and are expressed as integer values. This means, for example, that, if for the four empirical variables, indicators or items (a-b-c-d) of the same question or intermediate variable, the options in columns 1, 1, 1 and 2 were chosen (three times the option "Yes, in most schools" and once "Yes, in some schools"), the total value of that respondent for that indicator will be considered as 1 ("Yes, in most schools"), which will correspond, in turn, to the level or category "Very inclusive". This was done to lend significance to responses at the moment of consolidating them.

- To obtain an overall result of the perceived level of inclusion per dimension, a count of responses was made according to the option chosen (1: "Yes, in most schools." 2: "Yes, in some schools." 3: "In almost no schools". 4: "I lack information."), thus the level of inclusion per dimension was obtained. The three dimensions were then added together to obtain the overall result of the perception of inclusion in the Province of Buenos Aires education system.

- In the presentation of data, the "overall" values indicate the number of responses given for that intermediate variable, and are also expressed as percentages.
- The different levels of inclusion are represented for each dimension in shades of the same color, ranging from deeper to lighter shades (from higher to lower level of inclusion).

6

GENERAL RESULTS

6.1. PRELIMINARY QUESTIONNAIRE

PROFILE OF RESPONDENTS

This section presents the results of the preliminary questionnaire, which makes it possible to know the main characteristics of those who make up the body of surveyed inspectors; this will serve to explore internal differentiations that contribute to the understanding of the perceptions of the various levels of inclusion and their dimensions. The characteristics have been grouped according to three criteria: that referring to personal data (age, sex, training, place of origin, etc.), role or position of the respondent within the Directorate for General Inspection, i.e. in the supervisory scheme of the Province of Buenos Aires, and, finally, their relationship with people with disabilities.

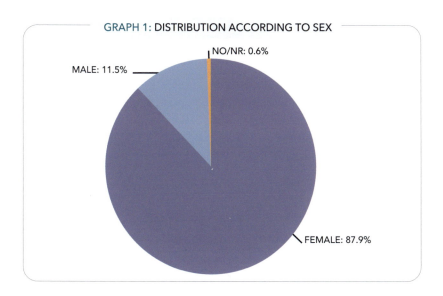

GRAPH 1: DISTRIBUTION ACCORDING TO SEX
NO/NR: 0.6%
MALE: 11.5%
FEMALE: 87.9%

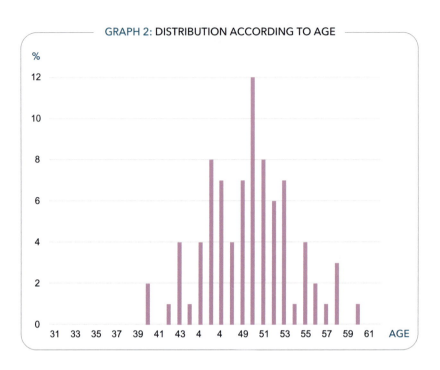

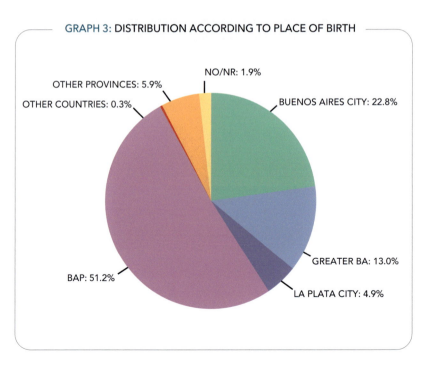

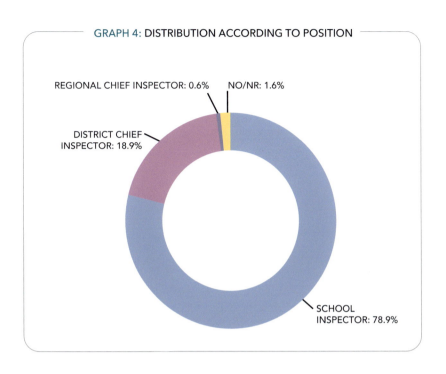

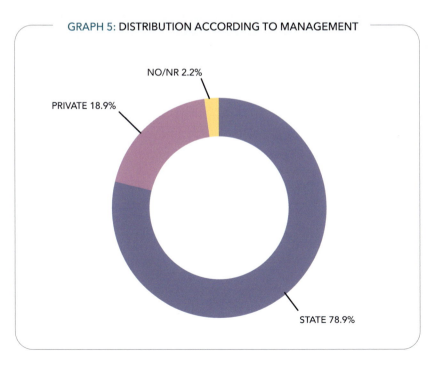

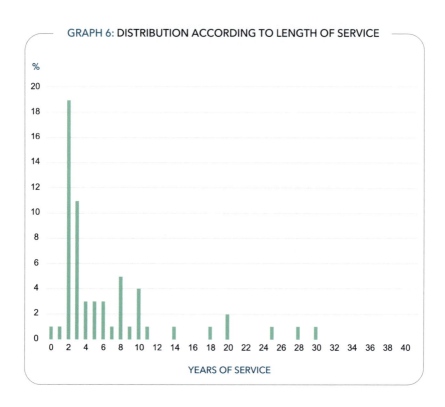

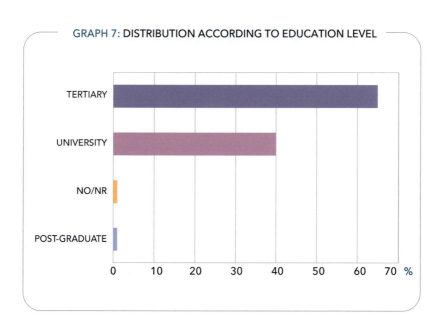

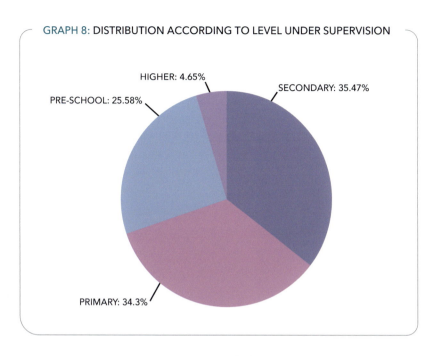

GRAPH 8: DISTRIBUTION ACCORDING TO LEVEL UNDER SUPERVISION

- HIGHER: 4.65%
- PRE-SCHOOL: 25.58%
- SECONDARY: 35.47%
- PRIMARY: 34.3%

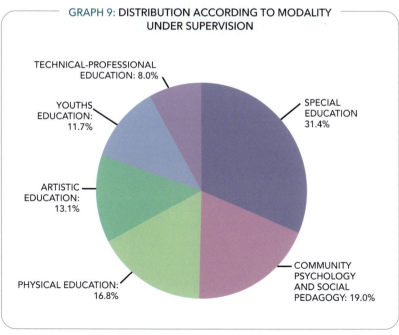

GRAPH 9: DISTRIBUTION ACCORDING TO MODALITY UNDER SUPERVISION

- TECHNICAL-PROFESSIONAL EDUCATION: 8.0%
- YOUTHS EDUCATION: 11.7%
- ARTISTIC EDUCATION: 13.1%
- PHYSICAL EDUCATION: 16.8%
- SPECIAL EDUCATION 31.4%
- COMMUNITY PSYCHOLOGY AND SOCIAL PEDAGOGY: 19.0%

Note: 13 respondents did not specify the Level or Modality to which they belong. These two graphs correspond to different subgroups within the surveyed population.

RELATION WITH PEOPLE WITH DISABILITIES

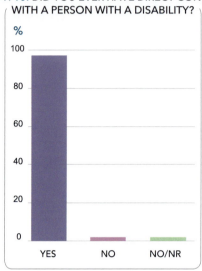

GRAPH 10: DID YOU EVER HAVE DIRECT CONTACT WITH A PERSON WITH A DISABILITY?

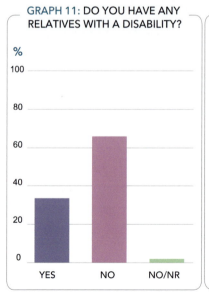

GRAPH 11: DO YOU HAVE ANY RELATIVES WITH A DISABILITY?

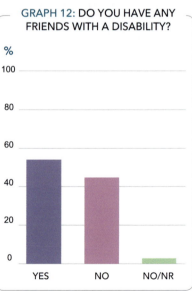

GRAPH 12: DO YOU HAVE ANY FRIENDS WITH A DISABILITY?

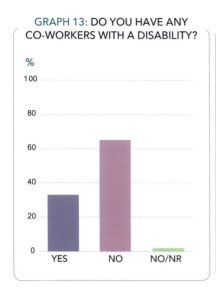

GRAPH 13: DO YOU HAVE ANY CO-WORKERS WITH A DISABILITY?

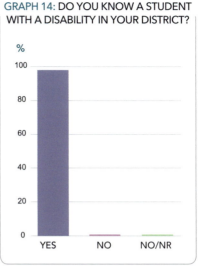

GRAPH 14: DO YOU KNOW A STUDENT WITH A DISABILITY IN YOUR DISTRICT?

The information collected on personal data (graphs 1-3) shows that the vast majority of inspectors are women, with a predominance of the age group ranging from 46 to 53, though there are some inspectors aged 30 and some others over 60. As for birthplace, there is a wide variety, with a predominance of the Autonomous City of Buenos Aires (23%), followed by the cities of La Plata, Bahía Blanca and Mar del Plata, but including a variety of locations, some of them distant, both in the Greater Buenos Aires area and further into the province.

Regarding their position within the Inspectorate-General (graphs 4-9), school inspectors account for 80% of respondents and District Chief Inspectors for slightly less than 20%, with a very low percentage of Regional Chief Inspectors. The percentage according to type of administration was 79% for state and 19% for private schools; and in terms of levels and modalities, the highest percentage corresponds to the primary and secondary school levels, and to the special educational modality, followed by Community Psychology and Social Pedagogy, and by Physical Education. The most frequently reported lengths of service are 2 and 3 years (20% and 11%), although some respondents report lengths of service of several decades (20, 30 years, and isolated cases of 40 years of service). In terms of education level, just under 60% hold a tertiary degree, 40% hold a university degree and only about 1% have completed postgraduate studies.

Regarding the relationship of respondents with people with disabilities (graphs 10-14), the vast majority (more than 95%) have some time had direct contact with a person with a disability and about one-third have a family member with a disability. The proportion of inspectors who have a friend with a disability is even higher (over 50%), and just over 30% report having a work colleague with a disability. Regarding their relationship with students with disabilities, almost all of them said that they knew one such student in their district.

6.2. GENERAL PERCEPTIONS OF INCLUSION

The majority general perception places the Province of Buenos Aires system at the intermediate level of inclusion, as only 47.3% of responses report the existence of items or direct indicators of inclusion "in some schools", followed by a perception of their presence "in most schools", which would correspond to a very inclusive scenario, followed by the perception of the third level of inclusion, that is, of a school reality that is "not very inclusive".

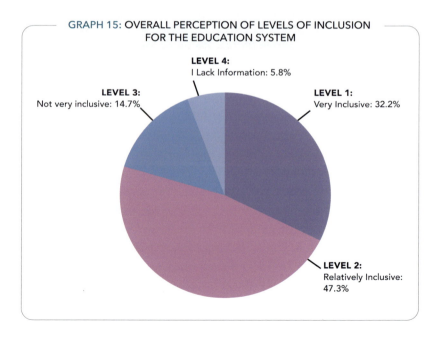

GRAPH 15: OVERALL PERCEPTION OF LEVELS OF INCLUSION FOR THE EDUCATION SYSTEM

LEVEL 1: Very Inclusive: 32.2%
LEVEL 2: Relatively Inclusive: 47.3%
LEVEL 3: Not very inclusive: 14.7%
LEVEL 4: I Lack Information: 5.8%

A revision and comparison with each other of the perceptions for each of the dimensions will reveal that the dimension ranking first - in terms of being more inclusive- is the one corresponding to "Producing Inclusive Policies", followed by "Creating Inclusive Cultures", while "Evolving Inclusive Practices" ranks third. It is noteworthy that the very same dimension of policies that ranked first for perception of inclusion should also be the one that received the highest relative response for the worst perception, which is explained by the 10-point relative percentage drop in the intermediate response.

GRAPH 16: OVERALL PERCEPTION OF LEVELS OF INCLUSION FOR THE THREE DIMENSIONS PROPOSED (COMPARISON)

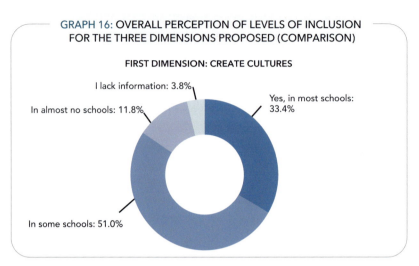

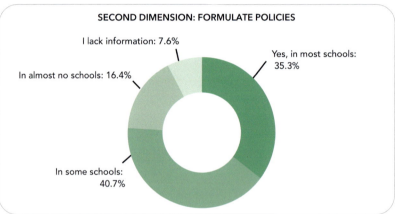

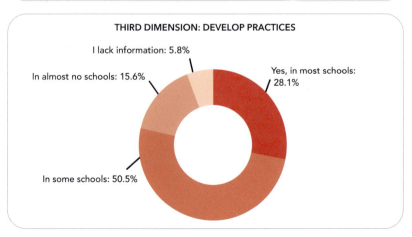

6.3. SURVEY QUESTIONNAIRE: VALUATION OF DIMENSIONS

6.3.1. FIRST DIMENSION: CULTURES

The analysis of the total number of questions referring to the first dimension, corresponding to "Creating Inclusive Cultures", reveals the majority perception of the level of inclusion corresponds to the second (intermediate) level, i.e. a system that is evinced as culturally relatively inclusive.

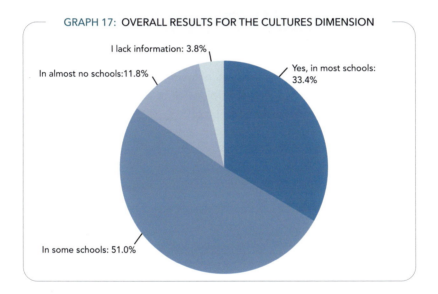

GRAPH 17: OVERALL RESULTS FOR THE CULTURES DIMENSION

- I lack information: 3.8%
- In almost no schools: 11.8%
- Yes, in most schools: 33.4%
- In some schools: 51.0%

A comparison between the perceptions of inspectors that supervise schools with private or state administration does not reveal significant differences; there is a slight prevalence of opinions of state-managed schools as more inclusive. However, the difference in the perceived levels of inclusion is more marked when the responses analyzed correspond to inspectors of different modalities and supervision levels.

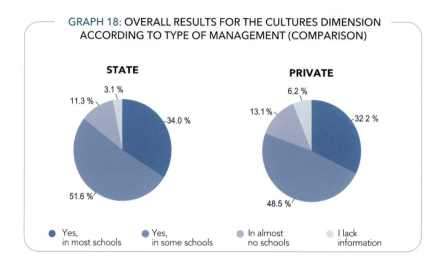

At pre-school level, the perception of 30.54% of respondents corresponds to the highest level of inclusion, a positive perception that rises to 37.5% in the primary school level, to become markedly lower as higher education levels are analyzed.

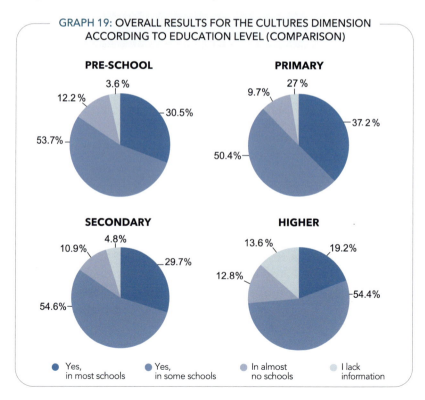

In terms of modalities, the inspectors of Youth and Adult Education are the only ones who rank schools at the highest level of inclusion. Technical Vocational Education ranks second for high level of perceived inclusion, while the remaining modalities do not show a behavior alien to the general situation for this dimension, so details are not included.

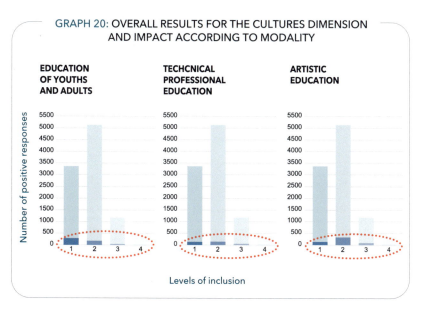

GRAPH 20: OVERALL RESULTS FOR THE CULTURES DIMENSION AND IMPACT ACCORDING TO MODALITY

Note: The bars show the total number of positive responses for each level of inclusion for all items of the questions in this dimension, that is, every time that the answer for each item of each question of the total number of respondents was 1, 2, 3 (levels) or 4 ("do not have enough information"). The red circles indicate the representation of inspectors of the selected modality.

As for the job position held by each respondent within the supervisory system, although this variable shows some differences in perception between school, district and regional inspectors, the results follow the same trend as the total for all three job positions. No different behavior is evinced.

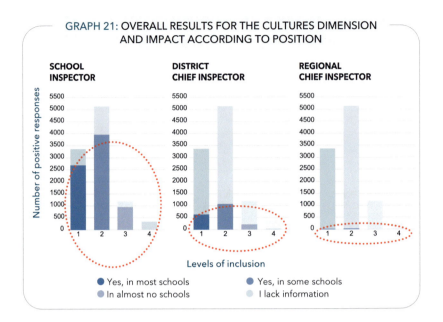

Explanatory note: The bars represent the number of positive responses for each level of inclusion in the totality of the items of the questions in this dimension, that is, every time that the answer for each item of each question of the total number of respondents was 1, 2, 3 (levels) or 4 ("do not have enough information"). Each type of possible answer/option corresponds to a bar, from 1 to 4. The red circles indicate the representation of the inspectors according to selected position.

Regarding the perception of the indicators proposed for each question or intermediate variable, the total results grouped for the intermediate variables or questions are presented below.

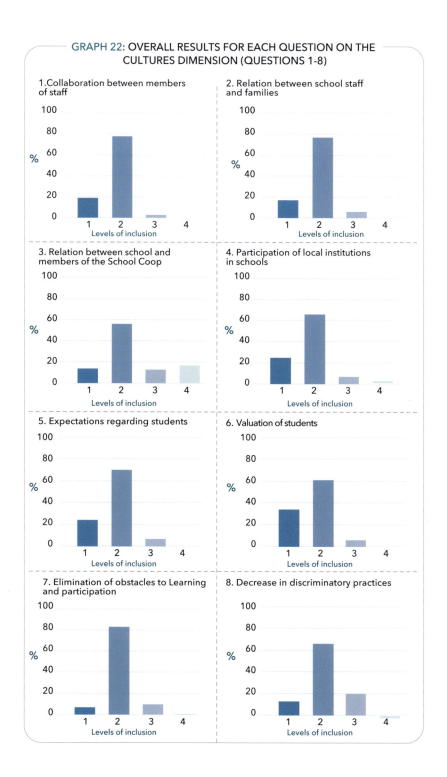

6.3.2. SECOND DIMENSION: POLICIES

Regarding all the questions referring to the second Dimension, Producing Inclusive Policies, once again the majority perception corresponds to the second level of inclusion (intermediate): a system with relatively inclusive policies, although this response appeared less frequently than in the Cultures Dimension, since for Policies the perception of inclusion grew proportionally for levels 1 and 3.

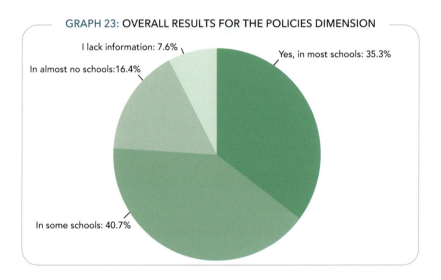

GRAPH 23: OVERALL RESULTS FOR THE POLICIES DIMENSION
- Yes, in most schools: 35.3%
- In some schools: 40.7%
- In almost no schools: 16.4%
- I lack information: 7.6%

The difference between the perception of results of inspectors at private and state administration schools is now negligible

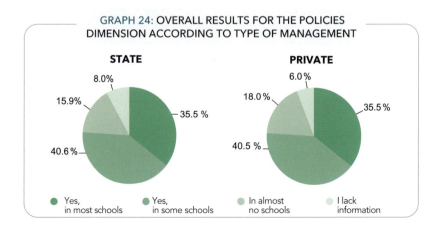

GRAPH 24: OVERALL RESULTS FOR THE POLICIES DIMENSION ACCORDING TO TYPE OF MANAGEMENT

STATE: 35.5%, 40.6%, 15.9%, 8.0%
PRIVATE: 35.5%, 40.5%, 18.0%, 6.0%

- Yes, in most schools
- Yes, in some schools
- In almost no schools
- I lack information

In terms of perception by education level, the percentages are in some cases reversed. For Primary School level, the majority of responses correspond to the highest level of inclusion, whereas for the pre-school level, the perception of inclusion is lower. This was also the case for the Cultures dimension for post-primary education levels, with a markedly lower perception of inclusion.

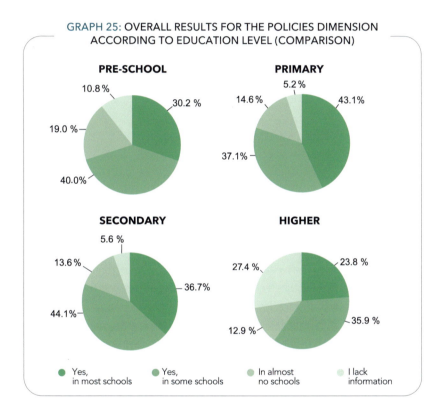

GRAPH 25: OVERALL RESULTS FOR THE POLICIES DIMENSION ACCORDING TO EDUCATION LEVEL (COMPARISON)

If answers are ordered by modality, once again, the inspectors of Education of Youths and Adults are the only ones to rank schools at the highest level of inclusion, albeit with a sharp 9 percentage point decline if compared with the first dimension.

Supervisors of Community Psychology and Social Pedagogy also assign the highest value of inclusion, although closely followed by the intermediate level.

The modality with the lowest perceived level of inclusion for this dimension is, again, Arts.

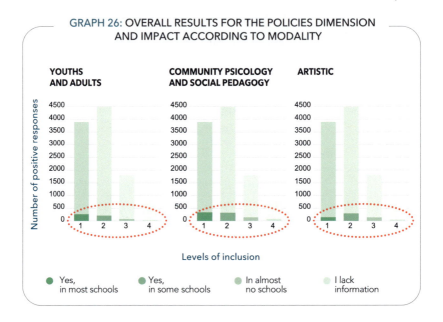

In terms of respondents' job positions, some differences in perception appear between school, district and regional inspectors. Compared to the Cultures dimension, where the responses of school inspectors showed a perception of a higher level of inclusion than those of district and regional inspectors, in this dimension, concerned with formulation of policies, the perception of district inspectors is slightly more favorable in terms of inclusion than that of school inspectors.than that of school inspectors. As for regional inspectors, the frequency of responses pointing to the intermediate level of inclusiveness is much higher, but much lower for the worst level of inclusiveness, level 3, so that their perception as not very inclusive is much lower in relation to Policies. It should be noted, however, that the sample is very small in terms of participation of Regional Inspectors, who account for 0.62% of respondents -only 2 persons.

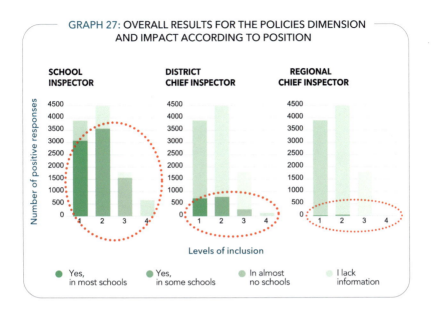

Regarding the perception of the indicators proposed for each question or intermediate variable of this dimension, overall results grouped together for the intermediate variables or questions are shown in the following graphs.

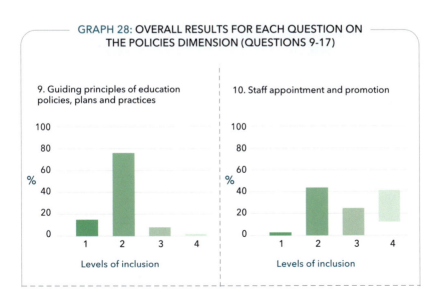

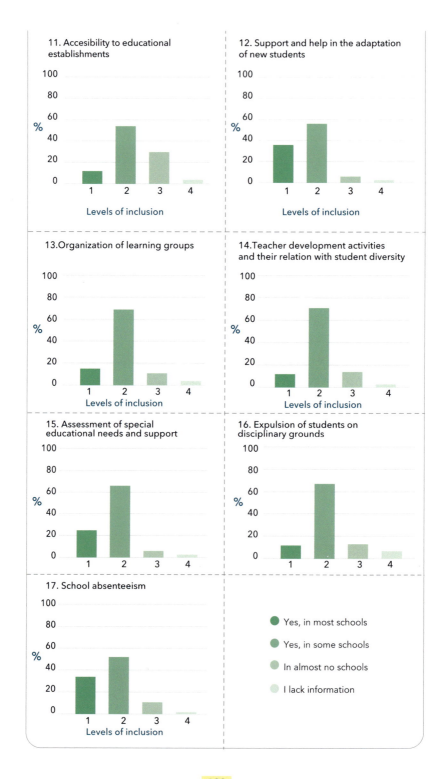

6.3.3. THIRD DIMENSION: PRACTICES

Overall results for the third dimension, Evolving Inclusive Practices, are the following:

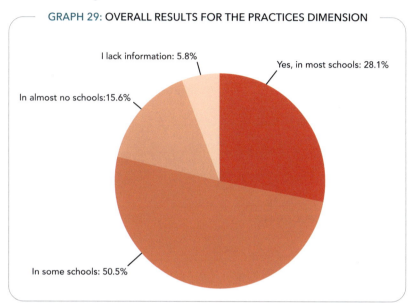

GRAPH 29: OVERALL RESULTS FOR THE PRACTICES DIMENSION

- I lack information: 5.8%
- Yes, in most schools: 28.1%
- In almost no schools: 15.6%
- In some schools: 50.5%

The difference of perception between Inspectors of state- or privately-run schools is almost non-existent, and the results in perception between levels are in line with the overall result, since, at all levels, moderate inclusion (level 2) is the majority perception, albeit with varying percentages.

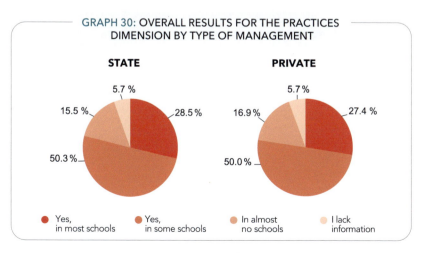

GRAPH 30: OVERALL RESULTS FOR THE PRACTICES DIMENSION BY TYPE OF MANAGEMENT

STATE: 5.7%, 15.5%, 28.5%, 50.3%

PRIVATE: 5.7%, 16.9%, 27.4%, 50.0%

- Yes, in most schools
- Yes, in some schools
- In almost no schools
- I lack information

Perceptions according to education levels show, in this dimension as well, that the higher the education level, after primary school, the more markedly lower is the perception of inclusion.

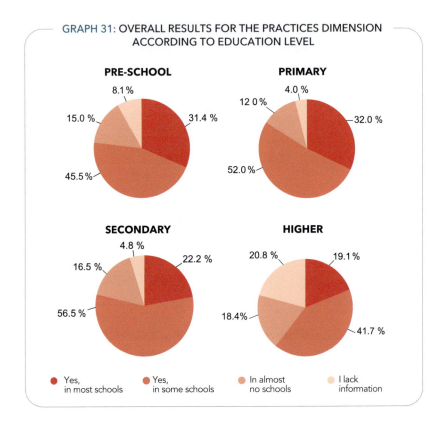

GRAPH 31: OVERALL RESULTS FOR THE PRACTICES DIMENSION ACCORDING TO EDUCATION LEVEL

In terms of modalities, as was seen in the previous two dimensions, inspectors of the modality Education of Youths and Adults rank schools at the highest level of inclusion. In turn, the low perception of inclusion of the artistic modality grows in this dimension.

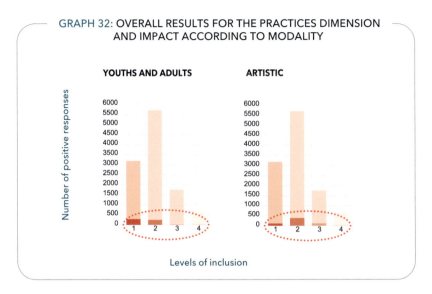

Explanatory note: Idem graphs 20 y 21.

With regard to the differences in perception between school, district and regional inspectors, the responses show a clear perception of a lower level of inclusion on the part of regional inspectors compared to that of the other two groups. In any case, the extremely low participation of regional inspectors in our survey is a serious limitation when it comes to drawing conclusions or making generalizations.

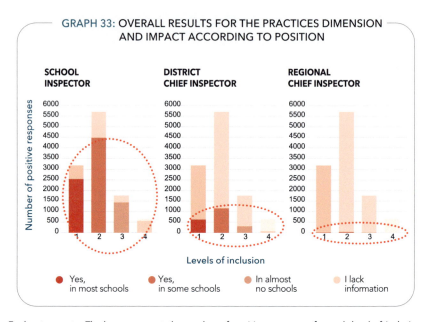

Explanatory note: The bars represent the number of positive responses for each level of inclusion in all the items of the questions of this dimension, that is, every time that the answer for each item of each question of the total number of respondents was 1, 2, 3 (levels) or 4 ("I do not have enough information"). Each type of possible answer option corresponds to a bar, from 1 to 4. The red circles indicate the representation of the inspectors according to selected position.

The specific responses for each intermediate variable proposed in this dimension are the following:

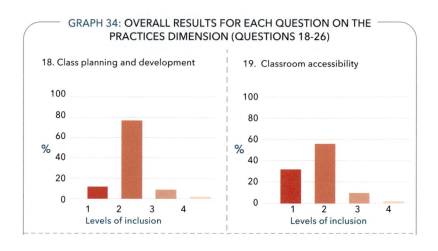

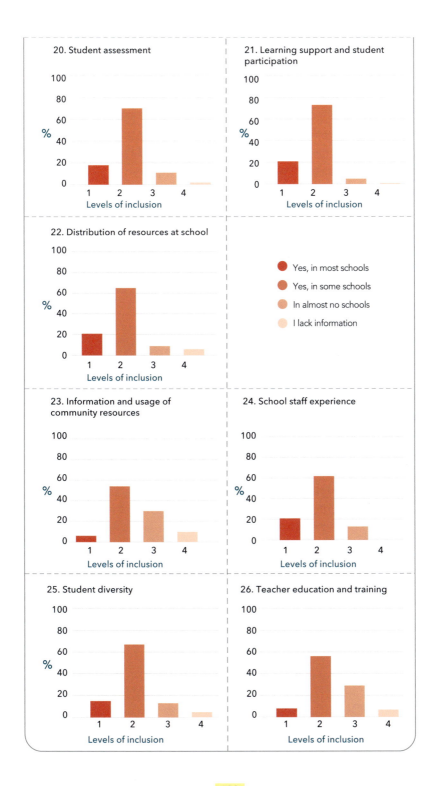

6.4. INTRA-DIMENSION CONSIDERATIONS

In general terms and on average, as the results above express, most responses fall within the second of the inclusion scenarios, i.e. that of a 'relatively inclusive' system in which the indicators or empirical variables surveyed are perceived to be present in some of the schools. This said -and before general considerations are dealt with- it is interesting to detect within each dimension those responses that deviate from the overall average for that dimension, i.e. those variables whose perception indicates a higher or lower level of inclusion in relation to the overall average for that dimension. It is also of interest to check their relationship - sometimes coincidence, sometimes contradiction- with other responses given for the same dimension concerning aspects that are connected.

6.4.1. EVOLVING INCLUSIVE CULTURES

In the case of Section One on Cultures, the responses obtained clearly concentrate in the second range of inclusion, which means that the cultures dimension is perceived by the majority of Inspectors as relatively inclusive. The second most selected perception for this dimension is the first level of inclusiveness (very inclusive).

When the variables within this dimension are reviewed, one question shows a result that is clearly at variance with the overall average: question 6 "Valuing pupils", which exhibits a clear preponderance of the highest level of inclusiveness. Let us look at the empirical variables at play for that question:

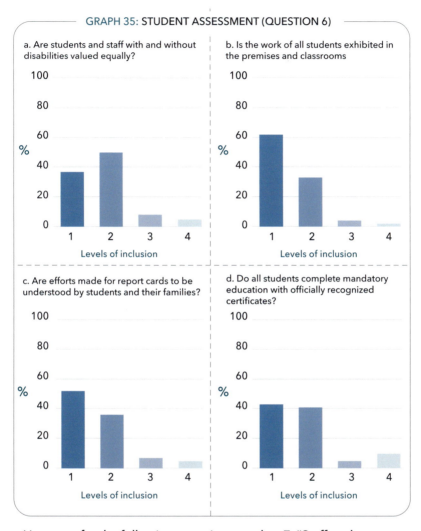

GRAPH 35: STUDENT ASSESSMENT (QUESTION 6)

However, for the following question, number 7, "Staff seek to remove barriers to learning and participation", there is a clear perception of a lower level of inclusion.

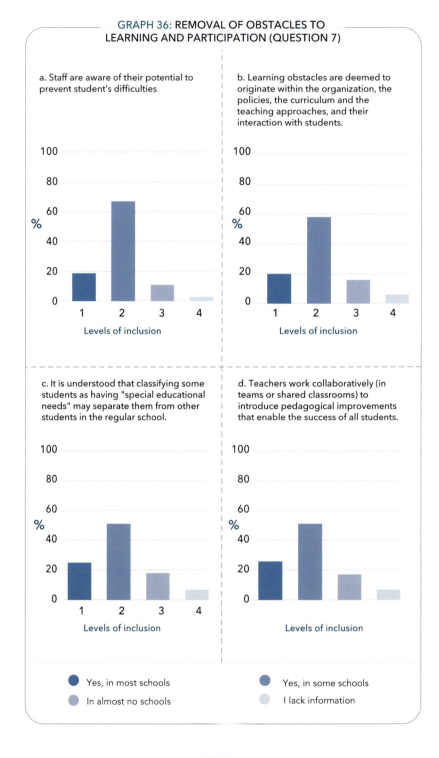

It is interesting to note the marked variation in perception between the two previous questions, especially when both refer to the position of the pupil in the school, albeit from different perspectives. It could be said that, on the one hand, the items relating to the way the pupil is valued (question 6) focuses on rather symbolic attitudes on the part of teachers and members of the schools (their valuation in terms of appreciation -not evaluation or assessment-, the exhibition of students' works in the school environment) or on aspects outside the specific decision-making sphere of each institution (such as the design of report cards and certification at the end of the mandatory education cycle, which are aspects regulated by the central authority). In the case of these empirical variables, their perception "yes, in most schools" implies a higher level of inclusion. However, in the following question (question 7), whose variables refer to mainly attitudinal aspects of school staff in connection with students' learning and difficulties, none of them has a high rating among respondents, most of whom admit that they are only present "in some schools": it is the recognition of pedagogical implications.

Section One, which deals with Cultures, shows in general terms responses with low level of dispersion and aligned with its overall result, with the exception of question 6 above, relating to "Pupils' appreciation", detailed above. However, there are two other items or specific empirical variables which, in isolation, are also widely perceived as being present "in most schools", and for these the system is presented as very inclusive: these are variables 3.a.

"The staff and members of the school coop know each other" (44.4%) and 4.d "Local institutions have a positive opinion of the school" (51.6%). This higher rating was given in isolation for this empirical variable (only one of the items) among those offered for the same questions (for the remaining items, the more frequent answer was level 2). The two questions refer to the link between the school and the community: the first one refers to the relationship between school staff and members of the school coop, and the second one to the involvement of local institutions in the school.

Just as these two items were considered differently (and independently) from the other items for the same intermediate variable or question, it could be ventured that, also presented in isolation, they do not provide much information about the inclusion in school of students with disabilities. They point to the existence of a harmonious relationship between the school and the community rather than to the inclusion of students per se. This is particularly so when it is considered that the other items were more specifically concerned with the type of relationship and reciprocal participation (valuing abilities, common approaches to disability, availability of resources, cooperation), all items more typically pertaining to inclusion processes in the strict sense of the term.

Below are the average results for each of the questions in the Cultures Dimension, according to the levels of inclusion. Question 3 (discussed above), and question 8 on discriminatory practices stand out here.

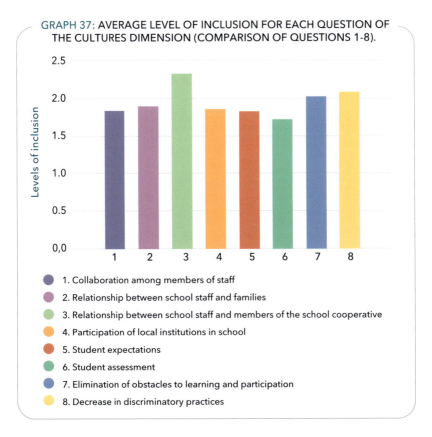

Explanatory note: The levels of inclusion are listed in descending order (level "very inclusive", level 2 "relatively inclusive", level 3 "not very inclusive", and the answer "I lack information" corresponds to level 4).

6.4.2. PRODUCING INCLUSIVE POLICIES

Within the second dimension of analysis proposed by Ainscow and Booth, the perception of overall inclusiveness is also in the intermediate range, though closely followed by the perception of inclusiveness at the highest level, which corresponds to a "very inclusive" system.

From the review of the results per question, the ones that stand out are numbers 17 and 10, with almost completely different results. Let us see:

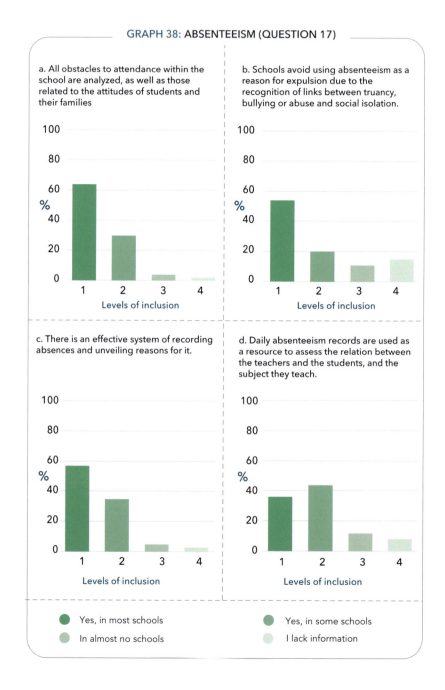

GRAPH 38: ABSENTEEISM (QUESTION 17)

In three of the items (a-b-c) responses indicate level 1, and only the fourth indicator shows the second level of inclusion (relatively inclusive). It is to be remarked that of the four items connected to absenteeism, the only one that shows an intermediate level of inclusion is the one that proposes a reading of absenteeism in relation to the connection between the teacher, the student and the subject taught.

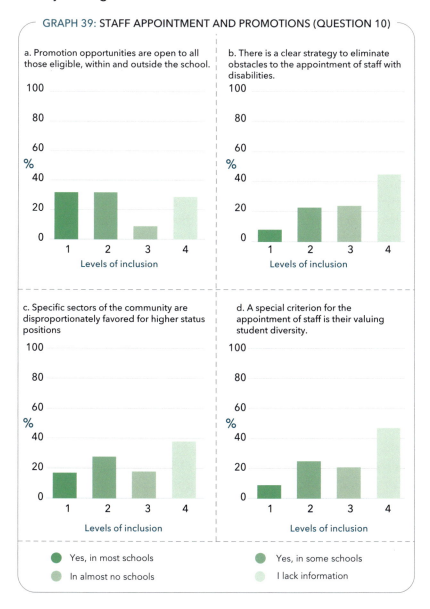

GRAPH 39: STAFF APPOINTMENT AND PROMOTIONS (QUESTION 10)

The following should be noted here: (a) This is the only question in the entire survey that shows number 4, "I lack information", as the second most frequent option (almost 30%). Moreover, option 4 is the most frequent one in three of the four indicators (b-c-d), where it ranks first for frequency. This is particularly surprising, since the issue of teacher appointment and promotion has a direct bearing on the professional life of respondents: although inspectors are located in the upper echelons of the teaching structure, a large number of them admit to lacking information about the appointment and selection processes (processes they themselves have been through). (b) The frequency of rating as very inclusive (level 1) is the lowest in the survey, not even 3%. (c) The perception of level 3 of inclusiveness (not very inclusive) is around 25%, with one of the highest frequencies in the whole survey for this level and the highest in this dimension (only second to question 23 "Information and full use of community resources" in the "Practices" dimension).

In general terms, this second section, dealing with Policies, presents responses with a greater level of dispersion, according to the different topics or points of the questions and the indicators proposed. It is to be noted that the responses to several of the intermediate questions or variables fall in the third position or lowest level of inclusion, i.e. the one that corresponds to a system that is not very inclusive, since it is considered that they are present "in almost no schools". This perception occurs mainly in questions related to staff appointment and promotion (question 10), accessibility of schools (question 11), and activities for the professional development of teachers linked to student diversity (question 14). Also noteworthy are results for question 11 and indicators a-b, related to school buildings and areas, and to the guidance and advice on accessibility that can be provided by organizations of people with disabilities: for both cases, the majority response (level 3 "not very inclusive") is above 40% and ranks first for this dimension, i.e. the one with the highest frequency for the worst level of inclusion. When compared to all the responses of this survey, only question 23 gets a higher rating in terms of high perception of very low level of inclusiveness (especially indicator d on whether adults with disabilities are included when it comes to supporting students).

In contrast to this, respondents perceive certain aspects linked to the guiding principles of policies, plans and practices to be very inclusive: among them, the existence of an inclusive and flexible curriculum (question 9, item a: 46%), but they place in an intermediate position ("in some schools") knowledge of regulations on the part of institutions (indicator b). When referring to the need to have a diagnosis of the student in order to gear education to their needs (indicator d), the most frequent answer is number 2 (50%) followed by option 1 (28.9%, "yes, in most schools"), which again confirms the presence of the medical paradigm of disability. Below is the average level of inclusion for each of the questions in the second Dimension, and the dispersion explained above.

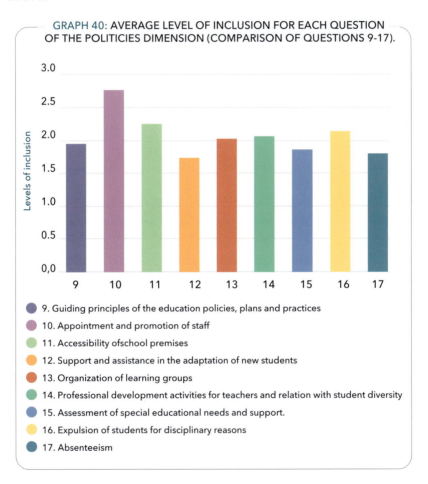

GRAPH 40: AVERAGE LEVEL OF INCLUSION FOR EACH QUESTION OF THE POLITICIES DIMENSION (COMPARISON OF QUESTIONS 9-17).

- 9. Guiding principles of the education policies, plans and practices
- 10. Appointment and promotion of staff
- 11. Accessibility ofschool premises
- 12. Support and assistance in the adaptation of new students
- 13. Organization of learning groups
- 14. Professional development activities for teachers and relation with student diversity
- 15. Assessment of special educational needs and support.
- 16. Expulsion of students for disciplinary reasons
- 17. Absenteeism

Explanatory note: The levels of inclusion are listed in descending order (level 1 "very inclusive", level 2 "relatively inclusive", level 3 "not very inclusive"; the answer "I lack information" corresponds to level 4).

6.4.3. DEVELOPMENT OF INCLUSIVE PRACTICES

Within the third Dimension proposed in our theoretical framework, over 50% of responses correspond to level 2 of inclusion, followed by level 1, and in third place comes the perception corresponding to a not very inclusive system. Questions 23 and 26, whose results per item are transcribed below, stand out as questions that fall outside this average:

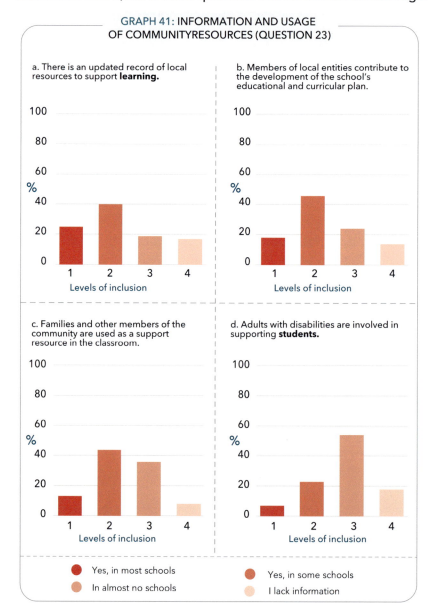

GRAPH 41: INFORMATION AND USAGE OF COMMUNITY RESOURCES (QUESTION 23)

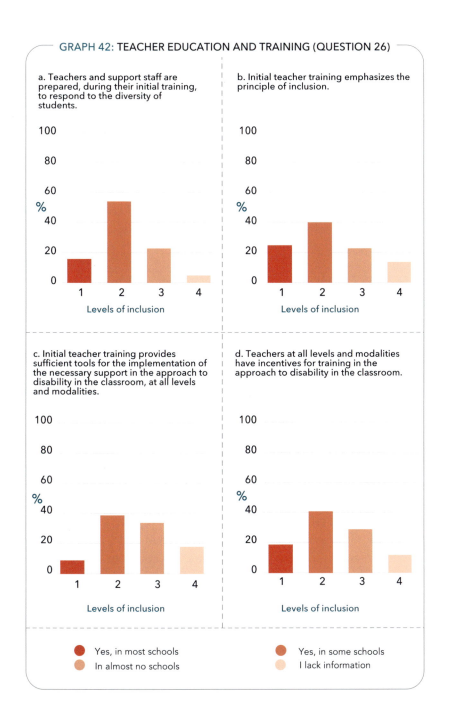

For both questions, the average result shows that the second most frequent response is the one corresponding to level 3 or "not very inclusive" system (close to 30%), while level 1 responses do not reach 8%. These questions are also of particular interest because they refer, on the one hand, to teacher training and, at the same time, to the full and effective use of resources existing in the community, so that it could be understood that, should there exist a low level of training in inclusion for teachers, schools could tend to compensate for this shortage resorting to resources from the community (NGOs, families), which does not seem to be the case.

Responses thus show, on the one hand, a lack of knowledge or lack of training of teachers and, on the other hand, a low level of use of other resources.

Section Three on Practices shows a clear predominance of the "relatively inclusive" perception on the part of Inspectors. However, for some indicators in particular, this perception becomes "not very inclusive", with a very high frequency of responses corresponding to level 3 ("not very inclusive"). In general terms, when questions are asked about information and use of community resources, what stands out is the absence of adults with disabilities as part ofa remedial teaching support system and, on the other hand, a serious deficit in teacher education and training.

Regarding the first point, this is illustrated by question 23, where indicator d is at the worst level of inclusion (53.7%), and question 24, where indicator d ("the staff of the special educational centers in the area interchange experiences with the staff of regular schools") is only perceived "in some schools" (43.5%), when, due to the organization of the system and resources (dual enrolment system until very recently, mandatory support on the part of the special school) should be a variable present in most schools.

With regard to the second point (deficit in teacher training), if question 26 is analyzed -"Teacher education and training"-, a certain degree of contradiction is apparent between its perceived indicators: while 53.45% of respondents consider that teachers and support staff are prepared during their initial training to respond to the diversity of students (indicator a), when asked whether initial training provides sufficient tools for the implementation of support to address disability, the frequency of positive responses for "some schools" drops by 15 percentage points (38.8%) and the response for the worst level of inclusion rises to 34.5% ("in almost no schools").

Below can be found a comparison of the average results for each question in that section, according to perceived level of inclusion. Here it can be seen that the worst average levels of inclusion correspond to questions 23 and 26.

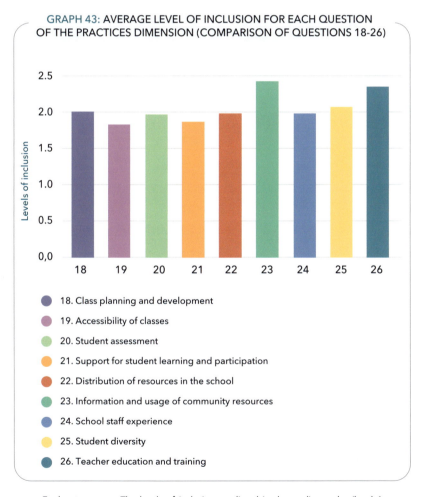

GRAPH 43: AVERAGE LEVEL OF INCLUSION FOR EACH QUESTION OF THE PRACTICES DIMENSION (COMPARISON OF QUESTIONS 18-26)

- 18. Class planning and development
- 19. Accessibility of classes
- 20. Student assessment
- 21. Support for student learning and participation
- 22. Distribution of resources in the school
- 23. Information and usage of community resources
- 24. School staff experience
- 25. Student diversity
- 26. Teacher education and training

Explanatory note: The levels of inclusion are listed in descending order (level 1 "very inclusive", level 2 "relatively inclusive", level 3 "not very inclusive", and the answer "I lack information" corresponds to level 4).

6.5. ANALYSIS OF COMBINATIONS ACCORDING TO LEVEL, MODALITY AND LENGTH OF SERVICE OF EACH INSPECTOR

Below are the overall results for each dimension, differentiating them according to the characteristics of respondents. Of particular interest are three general comparisons: firstly, responses according to whether they are school inspectors, district heads or regional heads, that is, those who occupy positions with different levels of responsibility and hierarchy; then, responses according to whether they are inspectors of the special modality, as this is the specific modality for students with disabilities; and thirdly, responses grouped according to length of service of respondents (above or below 15 years). Similarities and differences in their perceptions will be analyzed.

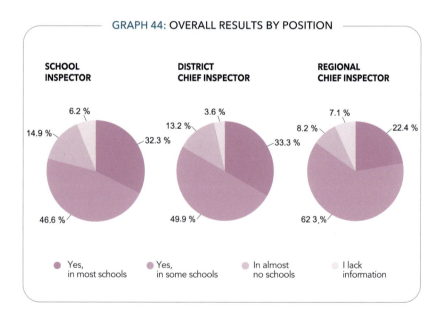

GRAPH 44: OVERALL RESULTS BY POSITION

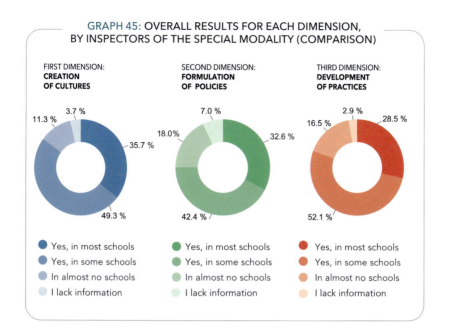

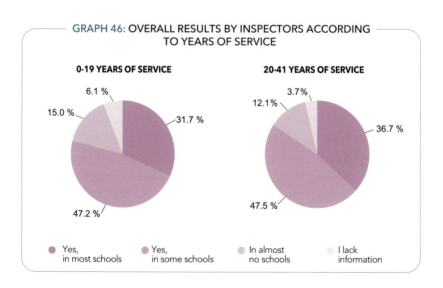

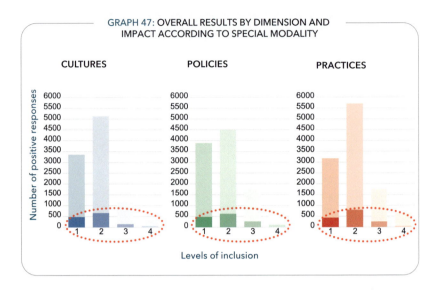

Based on the results shown in the graphs above, it can be concluded that:

A. For all job positions, the highest perception of inclusiveness (level 1, very inclusive) is in the Policy Development dimension (35.3%), followed by Cultures (33.4%), and in third place is the third dimension (Practices: 28.11%). This means that all those who deemed the system to be very inclusive ranked the three dimensions in the same descending order: Policies, Cultures and Practices.

B. In turn, with respect to length of service, it can be seen that as length of service increases, the perception of inclusion improves, so that those who have been longer in service perceive the system as more inclusive. This is possibly linked to the path people traversed through the system, as well as to their expectations.

Presumably, those who have been in service longer perceive the current situation more favorably than those who joined the supervisory system more recently (the former may perceive significant progress compared to the situation decades ago), and, on the other hand, it can also be assumed that those who have not been working in the system as long, have higher expectations in relation to inclusion and, consequently, their perception is less favorable.

C. The general perception of intermediate inclusion (level 2, relatively inclusive) ranks Cultures first (51%), Practices second (50.5%) and Policies last (40.6%). However, this intermediate perception varies according to the respondent's position in the supervisory system of the Province of Buenos Aires, as for each type of respondent, the ranking of these dimensions changes.

In the case of the perception corresponding to level 3, not very inclusive, the following paradox appears: the highest perception is in the Policies dimension (16.4%), that is, where the highest perception as very inclusive also appears (35.3%). This means that, as regards policy making, the intermediate range or level (level 2) drops -proportionally- towards both ends of the scale.

D. The distribution of perceptions of levels of inclusion also varies within the various dimensions, depending on whether it refers to school inspectors, district or regional heads.

E. It is also of interest to observe the perception of levels of inclusion for the Special Educational modality. As far as this modality is concerned, their highest perception of level 1 inclusion (very inclusive) corresponds to the Cultures dimension (35.7%), followed by Policies (32.6%) and thirdly by Practices (28.5%). Their general perceptions are within the overall averages for each level of inclusion and each dimension, so that no significant difference is detected among the inspectors of this modality if compared to the others. However, a slightly higher frequency than average appears for level 3 of inclusion (not very inclusive) in the Practices and Policies dimensions.

F. Responses corresponding to the fourth option ("I lack information") show a different distribution for each dimension, depending on the position of each supervisor in the education system. While school inspectors gave this answer for the Policies, Practices and Cultures dimensions in decreasing order (they indicated more frequently that they lack information on policies, while less frequently on cultures), the answers of regional chief inspectors showed quite a different tendency: they admitted lacking information on cultures (17.5%) far more frequently than in the case of policies (1.8%), and stated they do not lack information on practices (0%).

The latter is remarkable in one sense and to be expected in another: while regional chief inspectors are closer to the implementation and articulation of policies than to the specific dynamics in schools (it would therefore be unusual if they lacked information on Policies), it is not easy to explain their lack of information on Cultures (17.5%), while at the same time they do not mention at least a certain degree of lack of information on Practices (0%). Possibly, the general duty of supervision that weighs on them with respect to schools in general (and the eventual acknowledgement of non-compliance with them) took precedence when they answered questions about practices, and forced them to skirt the fourth response option offered "I lack information" (notwithstanding which, it should be remembered at this point that very few of them took part in the survey). This result was more likely, on the other hand, in the case of school inspectors -with direct contact with the schools assigned to them- who, however, admitted a lack of information in 6.2% of cases for Practices, compared with 8.1% for Policies and 4.3% for Cultures.

Overall, the fourth response possibility "I lack information" -and given the respondents' supervisory obligations- was left almost on the sidelines, with an overall incidence of less than 6%, probably because this statement might have implied (in the eyes of the respondent) the admission of some kind of failure in their supervisory work. There is therefore reasonable cause to suspect that, ultimately, the plausible responses have ultimately been limited to the first three options (very inclusive, relatively inclusive, not very inclusive), which, in turn, may explain the majority incidence of the middle option (level 2 inclusion).

This might lead to the conclusion that, possibly, in a new sample, the questionnaire should be reformulated in order to avoid the tendency towards the intermediate option, as the respondent might not deem the fourth one "acceptable".

The following is a synthesis of the data for the three dimensions, according to respondents' job positions and for the Special Modality, as mentioned above:

GRAPH 48: COMPARATIVE TABLE OF OVERALL DATA BY DIMENSION, ACCORDING TO POSITION AND SPECIAL MODALITY

Level of inclusion	Dimension total	CULTURES			Special Modality	Dimension Total
		Position	%			
Level 1 Very inclusive "Yes, in most schools"	33,4%	SI	34%		35,7%	35,3%
		DI	32,2%			
		RI	22,2%			
Level 2 Relatively inclusive "Yes, in some schools"	51%	SI	50%		49,3%	40,7%
		DI	55%			
		RI	55,6%			
Level 3 Less inclusive "In almost no schools"	11,7%	SI	11,8%		11,3%	16,4%
		DI	10,9%			
		RI	4,8%			
Level 4 NO/NR "I lack information"	3,9%	SI	4,2%		3,7%	7,6%
		DI	1,9%			
		RI	17,4%			

POLICIES				PRACTICES		
Position	%	Special Modality	Total dimensión	Position	%	Special Modality
SI	34,9%			SI	28,2%	
DI	38,9%	32,7%	28,1%	DI	28,8%	28,5%
RI	27,3%			RI	17,3%	
SI	40,3%			SI	49,8%	
DI	41,6%	42,4%	50,5%	DI	53,3%	52,1%
RI	63,6%			RI	69,2%	
SI	16,6%			SI	15,8%	
DI	14,4%	17,9%	15,6%	DI	14,1%	16,5%
RI	7,3%			RI	13,5%	
SI	8,2%			SI	6,2%	
DI	5,1%	7,0%	5,8%	DI	3,8%	2,9%
RI	1,8%			RI	0%	

7

CONCLUSIONS AND POSSIBLE CONSIDERATIONS

DIAGNOSIS: WHAT IS IN GENERAL THE LEVEL OF INCLUSION OF THE EDUCATION SYSTEM IN THE PROVINCE OF BUENOS AIRES?

HOW IS IT PERCEIVED BY INSPECTORS IN PARTICULAR?

WHAT ARE THE ASPECTS AND DIMENSIONS WHERE THE PROCESS OF INCLUSION IS PERCEIVED TO BE IN NEED OF REINFORCEMENT AND DEEPENING? PROPOSALS

The preceding chapter presents the general results of the survey, together with observations related to each dimension, highlighting some questions whose results were considered particularly relevant, while also noting certain variations. However, as expressed when the situation in the Province of Buenos Aires was described, the variations and differences between regions, between the Greater Buenos Aires area and areas further into the province, the different characteristics of its towns and population centers, the differences between state-run and privately-run schools and the different geographical locations, among other issues, present a diversity of realities that can hardly be encompassed in the presentation of data or presented in an identically uniform way for all its schools. Unfortunately, these (admittedly undeniable) differences between schools, districts and regions - differences possibly also present in the views and perspectives of inspectors - cannot be detected in this type of research. It is even possible to imagine that, faced with the format of a closed-options survey with three levels of inclusion, several respondents may have found the nuances unsatisfactorily insufficient. For this reason, it is imperative to make it clear that the results obtained are not intended to be uniformly interpreted for all schools and students in the Province of Buenos Aires. As already pointed out, neither are the results intended to be representative of the perceptions of the entire universe of inspectors, although they do have the value of offering an insight into the perspectives of a key member of the education system of the Province of Buenos Aires.

The preceding sections include comments on the results of this survey, detailing the variations not only between dimensions, but also according to some features of respondents, mainly related to their position in the supervisory system of the Province of Buenos Aires. A characterization is also made of the profiles of supervisors, profiles that, though not related in all aspects to the levels of perception of inclusion -this would warrant a much more in-depth and far too lengthy work-, make it possible to recognize the wide assortment of features (professional training, place of origin, age) present among them not only in terms of their position in the education system, but also of their personal characteristics and their personal links with people with disabilities (whether they have family members or friends with disabilities, for example).

The twofold objective of this work was clearly stated from the very start: on the one hand, to gauge the level of inclusion perceived by the body of inspectors of the province, in order to provide elements for a diagnosis of the situation of students with disabilities within the education system of the Province of Buenos Aires. On the other hand, the hope that this survey might serve as an effective trigger for change, not only in the sense of inviting the educational community to reflect on the educational situation of students with disabilities, but also - and especially so - as a pointer to those aspects that require substantial strengthening, those facets of the issue that should be the target of further work. In short, it is to be desired that the results of this survey shed light on priority issues and thus be useful for the design of large-scale inclusion plans and programs.

As a general approximation, then, the Practices Dimension is presented as a priority: it is the one that shows the lowest levels of perceived inclusion if one considers the frequency of responses for level 1. This dimension is the one most closely linked to classroom life and the pedagogical approach: issues such as lesson planning and actual lesson taught, support and encouragement of learning and of participation, and teacher education and training take center stage. The answers obtained particularly highlight issues such as the absence of adults with disabilities as members of the school support fabric. This is surprising in view of the fact that the majority of respondents (in the preliminary questionnaire) report being familiar with people with disabilities (a third of them state they have family members with disabilities, a similar number claim they have work colleagues, and more than 50% even affirm they have friends with disabilities). It would seem, however, that frequent contact with people with disabilities fails to extend to school life, as adults with disabilities are not part of school inclusion processes to provide support to pupils. Generally speaking, community resources are not exploited to the fullest: there is very little practical cooperation between community members outside the teaching staff, be they adults with disabilities or civil society organizations. It would seem (in line with the approach of the Sociology of Special Education, Tomlinson, 2012) that the organization of school structures is absolutely resistant to outsiders; those who make up teaching teams are -perhaps- jealously guarding their field of competence.

The question of teacher education and training deserves special mention, since the negative response rate (level 3) ranks second in the analysis of the tools provided by initial teacher training. It is poor when it comes to addressing the topic of students with disabilities. There is room to believe that, -as argued in the joint report to the UN (Edmund Rice International and Inclusive Education NGO, 2017)- the time may have come to design and implement a single and unified initial teacher education scheme that prepares teachers for the education of all learners alike, without differentiating between those with and without disabilities.

Regarding the Policies Dimension, what stands out is the positive perception of the national curriculum, as well as policies connected to student absenteeism and expulsion. However, the topic of staff appointments evinces a peculiar scenario, which might seem to reveal a certain degree of obscurantism or resistance to make the mechanisms of access to teaching positions transparent. In question 10, indicator a. "promotion opportunities are open to all", 22.4% of respondents indicated that they "lack information"; also for indicator b. of the same question on the appointment of staff with disabilities, the most frequent response -28.6%- was option 4, "I lack information". Along the same lines and for the same question regarding the appointment of staff, also for Indicator c. on favoritism, 35.4% of respondents gave as answer option 4. "I lack information". This admission of lack of information is doubly striking, given that respondents are precisely those who are at the top of the teaching hierarchy (and have therefore traversed its ranks themselves); not only that, they, in turn, participate in the processes of appointing school staff. The confession of a lack of information is therefore striking; it necessarily brings to mind Tomlinson's (2012) remarks when he denounces the existence of self-protection mechanisms on the part of those who make up the education system, a silent agreement of sorts, a kind of peaceful and concerted distribution of competences that admits the justification (and coexistence) of all its participants, within a scenario where inclusive education is still conceived as the new name for special education.

Continuing in the Policies dimension, the survey highlights a serious deficit regarding the accessibility of schools, the design of school buildings and spaces: Items a. and b. of question 11 show the worst level of perception of inclusion of the entire survey (between 40 and 42%). Besides, if a solution were to be sought, this reality is easily verifiable on the part of the political authority (as it is a question that can be ascertained by means of simple mechanisms); moreover, organizations of people with disabilities working to provide advice on accessibility could be consulted on the solution to this issue. Again, this is an interesting point for the design of an inclusion program that focuses on this specific point.

Finally, regarding the **Cultures Dimension,** it might be deemed an intermediate stage, the transition road leading from Policies (with the statement of its guiding principles) to Practices, which should finally have an impact on school life. Precisely, the level of perception of inclusiveness in this Dimension lies between those of Policies (with the best perception) and of Practices (the worst perceived level). The perception perceived for Cultures reveals the need to reinforce work for the development of more inclusive cultures within the system and, in particular, for the involvement of all members of the community, understanding it not only in its strictly school dimension, but also in its social dimension. In some way, it seems necessary to curb the interplay of internal resistance and self-protection of the education system and of special education, in order to open it up to the other agents of the community, in the broadest sense. This may be the only way to gain more in-depth understanding of the phenomenon of disability as one of a mixed nature that leaves behind the medical concept and opens up to the understanding that the weight of the view, the participation, the obstacles and the spaces provided by the environment towards this population constitute either facilitators of inclusion or elements that accentuate and exacerbate the segregation and limitations of students with disabilities.

• • •

As a **general conclusion**, then, it could be said that, according to the general view of the school inspectors surveyed, the education system of the Province of Buenos Aires is relatively inclusive and that the dimension of Policies appears as more advanced in terms of inclusion than that of Cultures, while the area of Practices is the one lagging furthest behind. In the light of the categories and proposals of the theoretical framework of this study, of the works that constitute the state-of-the-art and that collect information on school inclusion in other parts of the world, and of the reports of Civil Society Organizations also referenced, it can be concluded that:

- Results reveal a poor and meagre level of cooperation between schools and the community at large. Even when there exist social resources in the community that could contribute to the improvement of school inclusion, a strong absence has been detected of collaborative efforts involving members of the community outside the education system proper: adults with disabilities, organizations or associations, and even members of the families of students with disabilities. This circumstance coincides with one of the characteristics denounced by Tomlinson (2012) for special education, namely the very limited intervention of parents in their children's school learning processes.
- Results also show a perceived lack of general teacher training that is adequate for catering for the needs of students with disabilities. This

is also vital for the design of new policies: just as a larger number of "support" teachers, therapists and specialists, far from acting as facilitator of inclusion, act as a hindrance (Sánchez, Rodríguez and Sandoval, 2019), more training and the honing of skills is needed by all teachers, so that they are prepared to deal with all types of students, including those with disabilities. A single and universal initial training scheme of teachers seems therefore necessary.

- The design of the aforementioned scheme must be based on the conviction that access to one and the same basic education in the ordinary shared mainstream school is a right for all, just as is the obligation to attend school and complete basic education (Halinen and Järvinen, 2018); a rights-based perspective seems therefore appropriate. This civic education may need to target the community as a whole. In that sense, mass information campaigns may be useful.

- The need for all children to effectively attend their school of residence on a daily basis requires the cooperation of other members of the community, including their families, and the elimination of all obstacles that impinge upon this. Work on accessibility in terms of location, distances and school spaces is, again, vital.

- Cooperation within and outside the school is also linked to the opening up of schools and their assessment processes, as well as to initial teacher training. The design of a general system with a sub-system for special education, and in particular the absence of data and surveys for this sub-system (denounced by NGOs), flout the chances of greater inclusion of students with disabilities. The same is true for initial teacher training, which separately trains (and qualifies) teachers for typically developing children and other teachers for children with disabilities.

- Opening up to the community, cooperation between members and external agents and training for an assorted body of students means reducing isolation and agreeing to being observed. This, in turn, requires of teachers and school authorities the exercise of a new kind of leadership focused on action, co-operation and accountability for performance. This should be incorporated into specific plans and programs.

8

CONCLUDING CONSIDERATIONS: A PROPOSAL FOR CHANGE

Up to this point, the main theoretical issues at stake have been put forward, the survey has been presented of the levels of inclusion as perceived by the body of inspectors for each dimension, and some considerations have been offered on these results in an attempt to make an analysis that not only makes it possible to explain positions, but also to detect aspects that enable the development of new plans. It is now necessary to offer a concluding general thought on the perception of inclusion detected and the possibilities of rethinking strategies to improve the level of inclusion in the education system of the Province of Buenos Aires. That is to say, as Ainscow and Booth (2002b) propose that the application of their index and the results obtained lead to a true process of transformation in terms of inclusion, in this case, in the largest school district in Argentina.

The initial step to do this is to acknowledge the existence of an expectation that was not reflected in the results of this survey. By this is meant that the idea that the perception of inclusion might show significant differences between the responses of inspectors of the Special Educational modality, on the one hand, and the perception of the other supervisors of the system. These differences might be perceiving a higher degree of inclusion (level 1) eventually in defense of their own work within the fabric of education (in support of access to school education of children with disabilities within the general system, regardless of whether in segregated or in mainstream schools), or in terms of perceiving a lower level of inclusion (level 3) due to higher expectations concerning the students because of their own professional training, the starting point of which is a worldview more closely linked -at least aspirationally- to the pedagogy of difference and the valuation of neurodiversity. However, neither of the expected scenarios is confirmed: the perception of inclusion on the part of special education supervisors surveyed is perfectly aligned with the perception of the rest of the members of the education system. Their overall view of the school inclusion process does not seem to be influenced by either their training or the actual performance of their duties.

Reflecting on this result in the light of the specific theoretical framework of the author - both through the lens of the Index Code and of the Sociology of Special Education -and as mentioned above-, it becomes clear that this result should not be considered surprising, given that teachers, schools and inspectors of Special Education are but part of a general system in which the different educational modalities must coexist in an appropriate balance, and where each of them occupies a place, has a role and functions that are not in dispute: they coexist in the educational organization on the basis of agreements as to the competence of each, and with a clear definition of the scope of action of each. Possibly, the observation and evaluation of the particular situation of students with disabilities within the education system and their valuation in terms of higher or lower level of inclusion, and in the face of the growing movement demanding increased inclusiveness, opens up the debate concerning the reasonableness and/or justification of the existence, in the 21st century, of special schools (as segregated areas of education). What is implied by this is that, possibly, the perception of inclusion of students with disabilities as moderate, not only in the general but also in the special education system, can be understood as a game in which each participant in the system attends to their own position. And when this agent is called upon to assess that which is specific of other participants, they take a stand that is moderate, distant from either extreme that could be understood as a critical view that might enable bringing roles and competences under question, or even start off a general movement of reorganization likely to ultimately pose a threat to several other participants.

As long as the special educational modality provides support to students with disabilities, attention is not focused on "regular" teachers (whether the students are educated in special or mainstream schools); thus, it would seem that this allotment of students (after certification of their limitations, and justified by the "expert knowledge" of the professionals linked to the modality), roles and responsibilities, contributes to the balance for the harmonious coexistence of the various participants, without the specter of threats. This brings to mind Tomlinson's words:

> "Much of what happens in social life is the product of power struggles and vested interests, and special education is no exception. Each of the professional groups involved in referring, assessing, recognizing, treating, teaching or administering in special education has its own vested interests, its own sphere of competence and a variety of powers. The people who are involved in special education are in the position to mystify others particularly as special education is one of the most secret areas of education in which 'confidential files' are the rule rather than the exception." (Tomlinson, 2012, p. 8)

It should be recalled that -as mentioned above- in the face of the interplay of professional interests that can be detected particularly in the field of special education, the researchers of the Index Code team go so far as to suggest that it is impossible to redefine the field of inclusive education from within: they explain that it is precisely those coming from this field who generally understand inclusive education simply as the new name for Special Education, thereby failing to reflect in-depth (necessary though this is) on the further- reaching phenomenon of school inclusion and exclusion (Booth and Ainscow, 1998).

The possible revision of the given scenario (which most certainly extends to special schools) of the roles and functions of a sector (at least that of special education) can be - and probably is - understood as an additional factor of instability and uncertainty, in a post-modern world characterized precisely by the end of certainties and by permanent change and instability. We live in the present described by Benasayag (2013), where the myth of the individual and the unfulfilled promises of progress confront us with an evanescent fragile reality, in which man positions himself in a world outside himself that he considers hostile, but also does so on the basis of an inner fragility undermined by sad passions that prevent him from aspiring to the ideal of freedom, domination and control of days gone.

To escape from this mindset and to think of a different praxis that develops life, we must first of all begin by understanding the very essence of the phenomenon of life... The concept that best encompasses this essence is that of 'fragility', associated with that of potency. (Benasayag, 2013, p. 117, translation ours).

The idea of the social and individual need to hold on to the drive for life and (in order to make it possible) to embrace fragility as potency becomes even more evident in the face of the phenomenon of disability: from an individual approach, through treatments born of the medical model of disability, attempts are made to help or even cure the patient, but from the standpoint of the shared scenario, the actual purpose of work is to relieve society of the discomfort that the patient causes. As the author himself explains, now agreeing with Schmidt (Benasayag and Schmidt, 2010), although these two paths seem identical, their possible collusion poses a problem. The goal of eliminating personal suffering does not justify working to erase differences, because such existential suffering does not stem from the differences but from the intolerance of society. The balance of culture depends on people's ability to accept the existence of non-knowledge, to shake off the illusion of omnipotence, and to bring the full inclusion of people with disabilities from the realm of what is feasible to the world of what is conceivable.

These uncertainties and instabilities, together with the exacerbation of the circulation of information (now infodemics), also show -as could not fail to be the case- their impact on the world of education: Postman (1994; 2011) postulates not only the end of that invention that was childhood, which gave way before the unveiling of the secrets of the adult world, but also the end of education as it was known. In a current school scenario undermined by the generalized questioning of the institution of the school and the expansion of proposals in favor of de-schooling (Aldrich's book, 2011, is a simple and forceful example of the criticisms in vogue), Simons and Masschelein (2014) propose its revaluation from a perspective that seems to have been lost as a result of the phenomenon of the domestication of the school: that of the public space as a liberating one that makes differences possible and fosters growth. It is that school in which the role of the teacher is to sound the alarm clock at every lesson, in which teachers and students reflect on themselves detached from the context that ties them to a specific place (even detached from their background, intelligence and talents) that is the necessary school, in so far as "the main and most important act that makes school what it is has to do with the suspension of a purported unequal natural order" (p. 28). (translation ours). The school is -or rather, must once again be- that locus of time and space that allows students to steer away from the personal and community socio-economic order, to spend an egalitarian time that transforms everything into play, where the self is suspended precisely to enable the world and reality to become the object of practice and study, disassociating them from their proper use. According to these authors, these are the processes of politicization of the school (as tasks are assigned to it that are alien to what the school actually is, under a criterion of usability), its becoming family (teachers substituting for absentee parents and taking on the role of nanny that is alien to them), its naturalization (with criteria of differentiation based on talent), its technologization (a good teacher and a good school are judged according to school technique), its psychologization (which lays emphasis on the students´ emotional well-being and motivation, instead of calling them away from their psychological universe to become interested, precisely in what is external and foreign to them, and thus become students) and the process of making school popular (which focuses on relaxation and the pleasure of seeing and hearing, thus leaving aside the tension required by study and practice), which generated and lodged in society the concept of school domestication (Simons and Masschelein, 2014). This domestication of the school, coupled with teacher domestication, has today ultimately deprived the school of its basic social importance: the experience of 'being able to' that rejects the idea of a predestined fate, that space where anyone can rise above themselves and that offers the world as a common good that belongs to all and admits no privileged owners.

Perhaps, then, it is necessary to reflect more in-depth on the purpose of school (purpose understood as mission) to enable progress in the processes of inclusion of students with disabilities, so that the place to be held by students with disabilities is understood, defined and agreed upon. To think, among other things, of a school (and a society) that, having overcome the Foucauldian description, steps away from school domestication and rises as, again in terms of Simons and Masschelein (2014), defense of the school as a public issue.

It is necessary to start this in-depth review of the place in school of students with disabilities. The overall results that indicate that those who make up the inspection team of schools in the Province of Buenos Aires perceive a moderate level of inclusion that does not seem quite in line with the presentations made by Civil Society Organizations. It would seem that while inspectors detect a moderate (therefore reasonable or acceptable) level of inclusion, those who occupy a different social space -as they are outside the education system- detect levels of inclusion that are barely tolerable. Of course, their roles are different: while NGOs are currently important agents of change, the school institution is under accusations of being stagnant and unwieldy.

The above, as well as the overall conclusions and general observations of this paper, may not do justice to many schools and teachers in the Province of Buenos Aires.

There are undeniable differences in administration, worldviews and daily school life between teachers, principals, schools, districts, educational communities, within the same districts, and also between educational areas and regions; there also exist different views on the inclusion of students with disabilities. For this reason, and although this is not a comparative study of education systems but a research on a single system, it may be concluded that it is appropriate to admit again now, in these final considerations (as was done when setting out the scope of this work), the coexistence of a variety of positions and opinions on what inclusive education consists (or should consist) in. In Booth and Ainscow´s words:

"Even if we did not step outside the borders of our own country, we already possess extensive knowledge of the existence of differences in perspective on issues of inclusion and exclusion between and within schools, between parents and professionals, between disabled people and the creators of legislation about disability, amongst disabled people themselves, within and between a variety of cultural groups and amongst academics and researchers (…). This knowledge of differences in view should ensure that we avoid two pitfalls of comparative research: the idea that there is a single national perspective on inclusion or exclusion, and the notion that practice can be generalized across countries without attention to local contexts and meanings." (Booth & Ainscow, 1998, p. 4)

It should not be forgotten, for example, that incorporating students with disabilities into the general education system (meaning their enrolment, be it in a mainstream or a special school) is not the one and only conception of inclusion; the incorporation of knowledge is also considered inclusion, and these two processes do not always go hand in hand at present (Aguerrondo, 2008). Hence, also, the need to assess and collect data on their learning (besides their participation). Quality control is nowadays generally carried out through standardized tests (PISA, Aprender) but their administration poses a veritable challenge in the case of students with disabilities, since standardization, by definition, leaves out diversity. Though -as already stated- schools should not limit their function to teaching/learning but should extend it to education in a broad sense, this does not condone the omission of all types of assessment and measuring of learning to which the system has accustomed the families of students with disabilities, families that are content with the mere fact the student with disabilities is accepted and enrolled (sometimes schools function as "day centers"), but have no expectations concerning learning.

It would be interesting, beyond getting to know this general perception, that the results could trigger a true process of educational improvement and innovation. In this sense, the very application of the Index could mean the beginning of work for greater inclusion, as it raises awareness and forces the participation and interchange of opinions, experiences and views of the different participants in the education system, possibly incorporating those who are not formally part of it. It may be necessary to do this more extensively, with a higher level of participation, and even through the application of this index by educational regions, so that this experience enables an intra-system dialogue. A publication of results by region that would allow for the subsequent interchange of opinions and the involvement of other participants: not only inspectors, but also principals, teachers and students' families. Perhaps, the interplay of perceptions of the various participants will make it possible not only to correct individual distortions, but also to promote specific proposals in each school of the province. To this end, the three dimensions of analysis may prove useful to detect the first focal points of attention.

Following Halinen and Järvinen (2008) and their review of inclusive education policies implemented in Finland, in order to enhance the level of inclusion in the Province of Buenos Aires, it may be of interest to apply sequentially different stages of development: policies, educational structures, curricula, teacher training and effective implementation of instruction, with support, wellbeing and assessment. All of these elements are connected to some of the dimensions of analysis, with varying levels of perceived inclusion: while policies (to which curriculum design and student assessment are linked) ranked higher for level of inclusion, initial teacher training, actual implementation of inclusion and effective support by other members of the community were rated lower for level of inclusion. The dimension corresponding to the development of inclusive practices is the one considered as being most in need of actions to make advances towards inclusion, the one that requires the highest level of intervention for the implementation of effective inclusion. Thus, immediate and in-depth work on pedagogical activity seems indispensable, because, as Mitchell, Lange and Xuan Thuy (2008) point out, the work of teachers is an essential aspect of the implementation process. However, in view of the magnitude of the education system of the Province of Buenos Aires, it seems necessary to involve the inspection team and, in the case of supervisors -especially School Inspectors, since they are closest to the decentralized level and therefore to the daily happenings at school-, they should be made true leaders of the system, in Hopkins' (2008) terms. For the selection of personnel to fill this position, special consideration should be given to the performance of applicants to the position of school principals in terms of school performance (not only educational results in standardized assessments, but also in general inclusion issues such as level of school dropouts and number of those who stay in school), effective inclusion of students with disabilities, and leadership. It would be the school inspectors, i.e. those closest to school life, who should take on the role of in-system leaders to pull change along.

In the case of the Province of Buenos Aires, a process might be designed of application of the Index at schools with participation extended to principals and families, in stages according to geographic organization of the education system, so that during a first stage, work should be undertaken by region (25), then by district (135), with results of this first application of the Index shared with the schools of each region for their own evaluation (stage 3). It would be interesting to contrast and share the perceptions of families, teachers, principals and inspectors as a means to shed light on issues that some participants might detect while other might fail to. In this implementation process, the involvement of associations of parents and of persons with disabilities is downright vital. The importance of taking the education system in its entirety, and not just one school, as the unit for evaluation resides in the fact that this is to be the unit of exchange, as, according to Aguerrondo (2008, p. 78): "the unit of exchange is no longer the student, nor the classroom, nor the school, but the education system as such, which, naturally means changing schools (what they are like) and students (who they are)". (Translation ours).

From the perspective of this work, it is, in any case, all about what, in the field of the philosophy of the imagination, Paul Ricoeur defines as utopia as opposed to ideology: both are ambiguous in the sense that in both coexist a constructive and a destructive aspect; besides, historically, ideology is foisted on to others (and was hardly recognized as one´s own), whereas a utopia was characterized as a defined genre that invites to an unreal locus (in the case of Thomas More, a city), a no place. From this no-place, reality can be looked at anew; it is a new prism that causes the given reality to appear as strange and thus lose its entire obviousness. In this way, it is the utopia -in the present case, that of the full inclusion of people with disabilities- that opens up the field of the possible to other ways of living. Utopia is thus what enables the development of new possible perspectives, and its constitutive role helps rethink social life (Ricoeur, 1986). This no-place poses, from the standpoint of the philosophy of education, old and new questions hinging upon the what (what is education, what is the school, what is the student), questions that are no longer put forth in search of definitions, but to unravel their existential side and, by reinventing their meaning, reinvent a more human type of life (Masschelein, 2011). The survey carried out provides the clues to set off on the journey: check the accessibility of the various areas of the school, active participation and interchange with other members of the community outside the formal education system, education and training of teachers so they can be in charge of a one and single, albeit certainly diverse, body of students; unified initial teacher training not branching off into regular and special, guidance and leadership aiming to ensure cooperation and responsibility for own performance; in short, working to concentrate the teaching activity in one and single school that is a place for everyone to enjoy full participation in the educational experience and in learning.

REFERENCES

9.1 BOOKS, BOOK CHAPTERS, JOURNAL ARTICLES

Acedo, C. (2008). Educación inclusiva. *Perspectivas, 38 pp.*

Acuña, C., Goñi, L. B. & Repetto, F. (2010). *Políticas sobre discapacidad en la Argentina. El desafío de hacer realidad los derechos.* Buenos Aires: Siglo XXI Editores.

Adrogué, C. (2013). Equality of educational opportunities at public primary schools in Argentina. *Education policy analysis archives, 21, 89.*

Aguerrondo, I. (2008). Revisar el modelo: un desafío para lograr la inclusión. *Perspectivas, 38(1), 61-80.*

(2013). El rol de la supervisión educativa en la gestión de las políticas públicas. *Educar, 49*(1), 0013-027.

Ainscow, M. (2007). *"Towards a more inclusive educational system: Where next for special schools?" Included or excluded? The challenge of the mainstream for some SEN children,* 128. London: Routledge.

(2017). Para comprender el desarrollo del Sistema Educativo Inclusivo. *Electronic Journal of Research in Education Psychology, 3*(7), 5-20.

Ainscow, M. & Miles, S. (2008). Por una educación para todos que sea inclusiva: ¿Hacia dónde vamos ahora? *Perspectivas, 38*(1), 17-44.

Ainscow, M. & Booth T. (2000) – UNESCO Oficina Regional de Educación para América Latina y el Caribe (translation into Spanish by Ana Luisa López for UNESCO). Índice de inclusión. Desarrollando el aprendizaje y la participación en las escuelas. (available at https://unesdoc.unesco. org/ark:/48223/pf0000138159 consulted April 10, 2018).

(2002a) *Guía para la evaluación y mejora de la educación inclusiva (Index for Inclusion). Desarrollando el aprendizaje y la participación en los centros educativos. Consorcio Universitario para la Educación Inclusiva. Universidad Autónoma de Madrid* (available at http://www.xtec.cat/serveis/crp/ a8901114/INDEX%20CASTELLAN O.pdf consulted May 2, 2018).

(2002b). *Index for inclusion developing learning and participation in schools. London.* Centre for Studies on Inclusive Education (available at http:// www.csie.org.uk/resources/translations/IndexEnglish.pdf consulted May 2, 2020).

Ainscow, M., Booth, T., & Vaughan, M. (2000). Índice de inclusión. Desarrollando el aprendizaje y la participación en las escuelas. *UK: Center for Studies on inclusive education CSIE.*

Aldrich, C. (2011). *Unschooling rules*. Greenleaf Book Group.

Álvarez Balandra, AC (2011). *El Index de Tony Booth y Mel Ainscow: una mirada crítica desde la investigación-acción*. Universidad Pedagógica de México, Revista Universitaria Number 08, pdf available at http:// educa.upnvirtual.edu.mx/educapdf/rev8/ alvarez008.pdf (consulted June 22, 2020).

Amor Pan, J.R. (2007). Ética y discapacidad intelectual. Universidad Pontificia Comillas.

Andrews, J. E., Carnine, D. W., Coutinho, M. J., Edgar, E. B., Forness, S. R., Fuchs, L. S., Jordan D, Kauffman M., Patton JM, Paul J, Rosell J, Rueda R., Schiller E, Skrtic T. & Wong, J. (2000). Perspective: Bridging the Special Education Divide. *Remedial and Special vEducation, 21*(5), 258.

Aravena, M., Kimelman, E., Micheli, B., Torrealba, R. & Zúñiga, J. (2006). *Investigación educativa I*.

Armstrong, T. (2012a). *El poder de la neurodiversidad*. Buenos Aires. Editorial Paidós.
(2012b). *Neurodiversity in the classroom: Strength-based strategies to help students with special needs succeed in school and life*. ASCD.

(2012c). Neurodiversity: More than Just a Good Notion. *Creating an Appropriate 21st. Century Education, 27*.

(2013). *Neurodiversity: Discovering the extraordinary gifts of autism, ADHD, dyslexia, and other brain differences*. Da Capo Press.

Artiles, A. J., Kozleski, E. B. & Waitoller, F. R. (2011). *Inclusive Education: Examining Equity on Five Continents*. Harvard Education Press. 8 Story Street First Floor, Cambridge, MA 02138.

Ball, S. J. (1994). *Education reform*. McGraw-Hill Education (UK).
(2012). *The micro-politics of the school. Towards a theory of school organization*. Routledge Library Editions: Education, volume 32. London. Routledge.

(2013). *The education debate (second edition)*. Bristol. University of Bristol, The Policy Press.

Bang M. & Vossoughi S. (2016) Participatory Design Research and Educational Justice: Studying Learning and Relations Within Social Change Making, Cognition and Instruction, 34:3, 173-193, DOI: 10.1080/07370008.2016.1181879 (available at: http:// dx.doi.org/10.10 80/07370008.2016.1181879 consulted May 27, 2020).

Baquero, R. (2002). Del experimento escolar a la experiencia educativa. La transmisión educativa desde una perspectiva psicológica situacional. *Perfiles educativos, 24*(97-98), 57-75. Mexico: Tercera época.

Baquero, R. & Narodowski, M. (1991). Normalidad y normatividad en pedagogía. *Alternativas, 4*(5). Tandil: Centro de Producción Educativa de la Universidad Nacional del Centro de la Provincia de Buenos Aires.

(1994). *¿Existe la infancia? Revista del Instituto de Investigaciones en Ciencias de la Educación, 3*(6), 61-67. Buenos Aires: IICE.

Barber, M., & Mourshed, M. (2007). Cómo hicieron los sistemas educativos con mayor desempeño del mundo para alcanzar sus objetivos. [McKinsey Report]. *Santiago de Chile, McKinsey & Co, cinde*.

Becerra, G. (2018). La epistemología constructivista de Luhmann. Objetivos programáticos, contextos de discusión y supuestos filosóficos. *Sociológica (Mexico)*, 33(95), 9-38.

Benasayag, M. (2013). *El mito del individuo*. Buenos Aires: Topía editorial.

Benasayag, M. y Schmit, G. (2010). *Las pasiones tristes: Sufrimiento psíquico y crisis social*. Siglo XI.

Benavides, M. (2007) La atención a los alumnos con talentos académicos: propuestas de adaptación curricular. *Revista Latinoamericana de Educación Inclusiva,1(1), 59-66*.

Bernstein, B. (2000). *Pedagogy, symbolic control, and identity: Theory, research, critique* (No. 4). Rowman & Littlefield.

Blanco Guijarro, R. (2006). *La equidad y la inclusión social: uno de los desafíos de la inclusión y de la escuela hoy*. Revista Electrónica Iberoamericana sobre Calidad, Eficacia y Cambio en la Educación (REICE), Vol. 4, N° 3

Bonals, J. & Sánchez-Cano, M. (2007). *Manual de asesoramiento psicopedagógico*. Graó.

Booth T. & Ainscow M. (1998). *From them to us. An international study of inclusion in education*. London. Routledge.

Buitrago Echeverri, M. T. & Lara Bernal, W. (2013). Reflexiones sobre las comprensiones de la discapacidad y la sociedad desde una experiencia en el aula. *Investigación en Enfermería: Imagen y Desarrollo, 15(1), 65-83*.

Caldo, M. J. & Mariani, M. (2020). El trabajo del inspector en el marco de políticas de reforma. El caso de la provincia de Buenos Aires, Argentina, entre 2003 y 2015. *Foro de Educación, 18(2), 171-190*.

Cappelletti, M. (1994). *Dimensioni della giustizia nelle società contemporanee: studi di diritto giudiziario comparato*.

Cappelletti, M. & Garth, B. G. (1996). *El acceso a la justicia: la tendencia en el movimiento mundial para hacer efectivos los derechos*. Fondo de Cultura Económica.

Carrington, S. B., Bourke, R. & Haran, V. (2012). Using the index for inclusion to develop inclusive school communities. In *Teaching in inclusive school communities* (pp. 341-366). John Wiley & Sons Inc.

Carrington, S. & Duke, J. (2014). Learning about inclusion from developing countries: Using the index for inclusion. In *Measuring inclusive education* (Vol. 3, pp. 189-203). Emerald Group Publishing Limited.

Carrington, S. & Elkins, J. (2002). Bridging the gap between inclusive policy and inclusive culture in secondary schools. *Support for learning, 17(2), 51-57*.

Castro-Rubilar, F., Castaneda-Díaz, M. T., Ossa-Cornejo, C., Blanco-Hadi, E. & Castillo-Valenzuela, N. (2017). Validación de la escala de auto adscripción inclusiva en docentes secundarios de Chile. *Psicología Educativa, 23(2), 105-113*.

Clucellas M. & Scaliter P (2011). Acercar la escuela y la empresa: ¿Es este el verdadero dilema? En LA, O., & GRA, I. balance y agenda. (available at https://www.oitcinterfor.org/sites/default/files/edit/docref/AyA_10.pdf consulted June 30, 2020).

Comenio, J. A. (1632-1998). *Didáctica Magna*. Mexico: Porrúa. (available at: http://www.pensamientopenal.com.ar/system/files/2014/12/doctrina38864. pdf)

Creswell, J. W. (2013). *Qualitative inquiry and research design: Choosing among five approaches*. Sage publications.

De Grauwe (2008) School monitoring systems and their impact on disparities. *Background paper for the Education for All Monitoring Report: UNESCO*.

De Grauwe & Carron (2007). *Reforming school supervision for quality improvement. Alternative models in reforming school supervision*. IIPE - UNESCO.

De La Salle, J. B. (s/f-1951) Meditaciones sobre el misterio de la enseñanza. Available at http://www.terras.edu.ar/biblioteca/5/PDGA_La_Salle_ Unidad_4.pdf. (1706-1952). Guía de las escuelas cristianas. *Bogota: Ed Librería Stella*.

Deppeler, J. & Harvey, D. (2004). Validating the British Index for Inclusion for the Australian context: Stage one. *International Journal of Inclusive Education, 8*(2), 155-184.

Drucker, P. (2011). *The new realities*. Transaction publishers

Dufour, G. A. (2007). El rol de los actores de nivel intermedio en el gobierno del sistema educativo argentino. Un estudio centrado en la ciudad de Buenos Aires y la provincia de Buenos Aires. *Documento de Trabajo, 24*. Buenos Aires: UDESA.

Duke, J. (2009). *The use of the Index for Inclusion in a regional educational learning community*.

Duran, D., Echeita, G., Giné, C., Miquel, E., Ruiz, C. & Sandoval Mena, M. (2005). Primeras experiencias de uso de la Guía para la evaluación y mejora de la educación inclusiva (Index for Inclusion) en el Estado español. REICE. *Revista Electrónica Iberoamericana sobre Calidad, Eficacia y Cambio en Educación*. 1-4.

Echeita Sarrionandia, E. (2006a) Del dicho al hecho hay un gran trecho. Easier said than done. *Revista Latinoamericana de Educación Inclusiva*, 29.

(2006b). *Educación para la inclusión o educación sin exclusiones* (Vol. 102). Narcea Ediciones.

Ehren, M. C. & Visscher, A. J. (2006). Towards a theory on the impact of school inspections. *British journal of educational studies, 54*(1), 51-72.

Ferri, B. A., Gallagher, D. & Connor, D. J. (2011). Pluralizing Methodologies in the Field of LD from "What Works" to What Matters. *Learning Disability Quarterly, 34*(3), 222-231

Filidoro, N. (2011). Nuevas formas de exclusión. En *Educación Especial. Inclusión Educativa. Nuevas formas de exclusión*. Buenos Aires: Novedades Educativas.

Flude, M. & Ahier, J. (Eds.). (2013). *Educability, Schools and Ideology (RLE Edu L)*. Routledge.

Forlin, C. & Loreman, T. (Eds.). (2014). *Measuring inclusive education*. Ciudad: Emerald Group Publishing.

Fuchs, D. & Fuchs, L.S. (1993). *Inclusive schools' movement and the radicalization of special education reform.*

(1994). What's "Special" about Special Education? A Field under Siege. (1998). Building a bridge across the canyon. *Learning Disability Quarterly 21* (No. 1), 99-101.

(2009). Creating Opportunities for Intensive Intervention for Students with *Learning Disabilities. Teaching Exceptional Children, 42*(2), 60-62.

Fuchs, L. S., Fuchs, D. & Bishop, N. (1992). Instructional adaptation for students at risk. T*he Journal of Educational Research, 86*(2), 70-84.

Fullan, M. (1993). *Change forces. Probing the depths of educationsy.* Routledge.
(2001). *Leading in a culture of change.* Jossey-Bass.
(2009). Large-scale reform comes of age. *Journal of educational change, 10* (2-3), 101-113.

González García, E. (2009). Evolución de la Educación Especial: del modelo de déficit al modelo de escuela inclusiva. En Mª. Reyes Berruezo Albéniz, S. Conejero López (coords.). *El largo camino hacia una educación inclusiva: la educación especial y social del siglo XIX a nuestros días: XV Coloquio de Historia de la Educación,* Pamplona, 429-440.

Gorostiaga, J. M. (2007). La democratización de la gestión escolar en la Argentina: una comparación de políticas provinciales. *Education Policy Analysis Archives/Archivos Analíticos de Políticas Educativas,* 15, 1-23.

(2020). ¿Hacia la regulación postburocrática de los sistemas educativos latinoamericanos? Un análisis del discurso de los organismos multilaterales de la región en el período 2012-2018. *Educar em Revista,* 36.

Gorostiaga, J. M., Acedo, C. & González, S. S. (2004). ¿Equidad y calidad en el Tercer Ciclo de la Educación General Básica? El caso de la Provincia de Buenos Aires. REICE. *Revista Iberoamericana sobre Calidad, Eficacia y Cambio en Educación, 2*(1), 0

Grañeras, M., Lamelas, R., Segalerva, A., Vázquez, E., Gordo, J. L. & Molinuevo, (1998). *Catorce años de investigación sobre las desigualdades en educación en España.* Madrid, Centro de Investigación y Documentación Educativa.

Gvirtz, S. & Podestá, M.E. (2012). *El rol del supervisor en la mejora escolar.* Buenos Aires: Aique Educación.

Halinen, I. & Järvinen, R. (2008). En pos de la educación inclusiva: el caso de Finlandia. *Perspectivas, 38*(1), 97-127.

Heung, V. (2006). Can the introduction of an inclusion index move a system forward? *International Journal of Inclusive Education, 10*(4-5), 309- 322.

Hirschman, A. (1970). Exit, Voice and Loyalty: Responses to Decline in Firms, Organizations and States (Cambridge, MA: Harvard University Press).

Hopkins, D. (2008). Realising the potential of system leadership. *Improving school leadership, 2,* 21-35.

John, J. D. (2007). Albert Hirschman's exit-voice framework and its relevance to problems of public education performance in Latin America. *Oxford Development Studies, 35*(3), 295-327.

Klingner, J. K. & Boardman, A. G. (2011). Addressing the "research gap" in special education through mixed methods. *Learning Disability Quarterly, 34*(3), 208-218.

Levin, H.M (2008). The Economic Payoff to investing in Educational Justice. *Educational Researcher*, 2009, vol. 38, n 1, 5-20. Available at https:// journals.sagepub.com/doi/pdf/10.3102/0013189X08331192 (consulted May 27, 2020).

Levine, M. D. (2003). *Mentes diferentes, aprendizajes diferentes: un modelo educativo para desarrollar el potencial individual de cada niño*. Paidós.

Litwin, E. (1994). La tecnología educativa y la didáctica: un debate vigente. Separata. *Revista Educación, 3*(6).

Lus, M. A. (1995). *El pesado tema del retardo mental leve. De la*.

Mac Gregor, E. F. (2009). Mauro Cappelletti y el Derecho procesal constitucional comparado. *Anuario iberoamericano de justicia constitucional*, (13), 267-306.

Maldonado, J. A. V. (2013). El modelo social de la discapacidad: una cuestión de derechos humanos. *Revista de Derecho de la UNED (RDUNED)*, (12)

Maldonado, L (2020). *Tecnología y Educación. Recursos para personas con dificultades de aprendizaje, limitaciones intelectuales, motoras, visuales y auditivas*. Buenos Aires. Ed. Biblos.

Masschelein, J. (2011). Philosophy of education. *Bajo Palabra. Revista de filosofía, 2*(6), 39-40.

Mead, M. (1970/2006). *Cultura y compromiso. El mensaje de la nueva generación* (5th. Reprint). Barcelona: Gedisa.

Mitchell, C., De Lange, N. & Thuy, N. T. X. (2008). "Let's not leave this problem": exploring inclusive education in rural South Africa. *Prospects, 38* (1), 99-112.

Moya Maya, A., Martínez Ferrer, J. & Ruiz Salguero, J. M. (2012). *Del aula de educación especial al aula de recursos. Una evolución hacia la inclusión*.

Murillo, J., Krichesky G., Castro A. & Hernández R. (2010). Liderazgo para la inclusión escolar y la justicia social. Aportaciones de la investigación. *Revista Latinoamericana de Inclusión Educativa*, 4(1), pp.169-186. Available at: http://www.rinace.net/rlei/numeros/vol4-num1/art8.html.

Narodowski, M. (1999) *Después de clase. Desencantos y desafíos de la escuela actual*. Colección Educausa, Buenos Aires: Novedades Educativas.

(2018). *El colapso de la educación*, Buenos Aires. Paidós.

Opertti, R. & Belalcázar, C. (2008). Tendencias de la educación inclusiva a nivel regional e interregional: temas y desafíos. *Perspectivas, 38*(1), 149-179.

Par, F. (2005). La discapacidad en Argentina. *Un diagnóstico de situación y políticas públicas vigentes al 2005*.

Perrenoud, P. (1990). *La construcción del éxito y del fracaso escolar*. Madrid: Morata.
(2004). *Desarrollar la práctica reflexiva en el oficio de enseñar: profesionalización y razón pedagógica* (Vol. 1). Graó.

(2005). Diez nuevas competencias para enseñar. *Educatio Siglo XXI, 23*. (available at: http://revistas.um.es/index.php/educatio/article/ viewFile/127/111).

Polat, F. (2011). Inclusion in education: A step towards social justice. *International Journal of Educational Development, 31*(1), 50-58.

Ponce de León, M. A. & Longobucco, H. J. (2008). Los perfiles profesionales de los inspectores de la provincia de Buenos Aires: Entre los cambios socioeducativos recientes y las trayectorias laborales y formativas. En *V Jornadas de Sociología de la UNLP 10, 11 y 12 de diciembre de 2008 La Plata, Argentina*. Universidad Nacional de La Plata. Facultad de Humanidades y Ciencias de la Educación. Departamento de Sociología.

Portuondo Sao, M. (2004). Evolución del concepto social de discapacidad intelectual. *Revista cubana de salud pública, 30*(4), 0-0.

Postman, N. (1994). *The Disappearance of Childhood*. 1982. New York: Vintage. (2011). *The end of education: Redefining the value of school*. Vintage.

Ricoeur, P (1986). *Ideología y utopía*. Barcelona. Editorial Gedisa.

Romero, C. (2004). *La escuela media en la sociedad del conocimiento*. Buenos Aires: Novedades Educativas.

(2013). *Hacer de una escuela, una buena escuela*. Buenos Aires: Aique.

Rovner, H. & Monjeau E (2017). *La mala educación*. Buenos Aires. Penguin Random House.

Rueda, R. (2011). Commentary: The need for more expansive frameworks: A practical perspective. *Learning Disability Quarterly*, 180-182.

Rutter, M., Tizard, J. & Whitmore, K. (1970). *Education, health and behaviour*. Longman Publishing Group.

Saccon, E. J. (2018). El derecho a la educación inclusiva, un título en igualdad de condiciones. *Derechos en Acción, 7*, 60.

Sánchez S., Rodríguez, H. & Sandoval M. (2019). Descriptive and comparative analysis of School Inclusion through Index for Inclusion. *Psychology, Society & Education, 11*(1), 1-13.

Sánchez Zinny, G (2020). *Educación. Lo que no nos cuentan*. Fundación de Promoción Educativa.

Sandrone, R. S. (2021). Construir la identidad del inspector de zona escolar en tiempos de complejidad. *Sophia, 17*(2), e1053-e1053.

Simons, M. & Masschelein, J. (2014). Defensa de la Escuela. Una cuestión pública. *Colección Educación: Otros Lenguajes*.

Sinek, S. (2014). *Leaders eat last: Why some teams pull together and others don't*. Penguin.

Skliar, C. (1999). *Educar a cualquiera y a cada uno. Sobre el estar-juntos en la educación*. (2005) Poner en tela de juicio la normalidad, no la anormalidad. Argumento y falta de argumentos con relación a las diferencias en educación. En *La construcción social de la normalidad. Alteridades, diferencias y diversidad*. Buenos Aires: Novedades educativas. Available at (https:// revistas.udea.edu.co/index.php/ revistaeyp/article/view/6024/5431 consulted October 6, 2021).

(2007). *La educación (que es) del otro: argumentos y desierto de argumentos pedagógicos*. Noveduc Libros.

(2009). Del estar-juntos en educación. *Revista Sul- Americana de Filosofía e Educação*, (12), 63-76.

(2010). De la razón jurídica hacia una ética peculiar. A propósito del informe mundial sobre el derecho a la educación de personas con discapacidad. *Política y sociedad*,*47*(1), 153-164.

Skliar, C. & Bárcena, F. (2013). Cartas sobre la diferencia. Una cuestión de palabras (entre la amistad, la incomodidad y el sinsentido). *Plumilla Educativa*, (12), 11-28.

Skliar, C. & Larrosa, J. (2009). Experiencia y alteridad en educación. (1 Edición) Argentina: Homo Sapiens.

Sosa, L. M. (2008). Educación corporal y Diversidad (estudio sobre prácticas corporales de inclusión de niños/as con discapacidades). In *Jornadas de Cuerpo y Cultura* of the *Universidad Nacional de La Plata, Facultad de Humanidades y Ciencias de la Educación, Departamento de Educación Física*.

Souto Simão, M., Águila Mendizábal, C. D., Alas Solís, M., Camargo, R. B. D., Castillo Aramburu, M., Martínez Ellsberg, J & Villalobos Dintrans. C. (2016). *Transferencias directas a escuelas: reflexiones sobre prácticas en América Latina*. (available in pdf at www: http://ceppe.uc.cl/images/articulo/ Transferencias_a_Escuelas_AL. pdf consulted June 30, 2020).

Terigi, F. (2009). *Los sistemas nacionales de inspección / supervisión escolar. Revisión de la literatura y análisis de casos*. Buenos Aires: IIPE-UNESCO, Sede Regional de Buenos Aires.

Tomlinson, S. (1982/2012). *A sociology of special education*. Abingdon. Routledge & Kegan Paul. London, Boston & J Henley.

(2014). *The Politics of Race, Class and Special Education: The Selected Works of Sally Tomlinson*. Routledge.

Torres González, J. A. (2010). Pasado, presente y futuro de la atención a las necesidades educativas especiales: Hacia una educación inclusiva. *Perspectiva Educacional*, *49*(1), 62-113.

Vain, P. (2005) Educación y diversidad. Espejismos y realidades. En *La construcción social de la normalidad. Alteridades, diferencias y diversidad*. Buenos Aires: Novedades educativas.

(2006) El concepto de necesidades educativas especiales ¿Un nuevo eufemismo educativo? In *Educación Especial. Inclusión Educativa. Nuevas formas de exclusión*. Buenos Aires: Novedades Educativas.

Valdez, D. D. (2009/2012). *Ayudas para aprender: Trastornos del desarrollo y prácticas inclusivas*. (3rd. Reprint). Buenos Aires: Paidós.

Veleda, C., Rivas, A. & Mezzadra, F. (2011). *La construcción de la justicia educativa: criterios de redistribución y reconocimiento para la educación argentina*. CIPPEC.

Verdugo Alonso, M. A. (2003). De la segregación a la inclusión escolar. In *Educar para la vida* (pp. 9-18). Obra Social y Cultural Cajasur.

Viñao F., A. (2002). *Sistemas educativos, culturas escolares y reformas: continuidades y cambios* (Vol. 10). Ediciones Morata.

(1999). La inspección educativa: análisis socio-histórico de una profesión. *Bordón. Revista de pedagogía, 51*(3), 251-263.

Vivar, D. M., Delgado, P. S., Corona, D. G. & García, M. G. (2011). De la exclusión a la inclusión: una forma de entender y atender a la diversidad funcional en las instituciones escolares. *Educación y diversidad. Education and diversity: Revista inter-universitaria de investigación sobre discapacidad e interculturalidad, 5*(1), 23-31.

Warnock, M. A. R. Y. (1979). Children with special needs: the Warnock Report. *British Medical Journal, 1*(6164), 667.

World Health Organization & The World Bank (2011), *World Report on Disability*, available at https://www.who.int/publications/i/item/9789241564182)

9.2. DOCUMENTS, TREATIES, REPORTS AND LEGISLATION

Adrogué M.J. & Septiembre Films (2010). *Oportunidades*. Youtube (ww.youtube. com/watch?v=18YcelJk2O4&t=39s)

Argentina - Estado Argentino (2018) *Informes periódicos segundo y tercero presentados por el Estado Argentino ante el Comité de los Derechos de las Personas con Discapacidad, de la Organización de las Naciones Unidas* (retrieved September 16, 2020 from https://tbinternet.ohchr.org/_layouts/15/treatybodyexternal/Downloa d.aspx?symbolno=CRPD%2fC%2fARG% 2f2-3&Lang=es)

Argentina - Ministerio Público de la Defensa, Defensoría General de la Nación Argentina (2017). *Informe al Comité de los Derechos de las Personas con Discapacidad, de la Organización de las Naciones Unidas* (retrieved September 16, 2020 desdehttps://tbinternet.ohchr.org/_layouts/15/treatybodyexternal/Downloa d.aspx?symbolno=INT%2fCRPD%2flCS%2fARG%2f28580&Lang= es

Consejo Federal de Educación (2016). *Resolución 311/2016 "Promoción, acreditación, certificación y titulación de estudiantes con discapacidad* (retrieved April 6, 2020 from https://www.argentina.gob.ar/sites/default/files/res-311-cfe- 58add7585fbc4. pdf)

Dirección General de Cultura y Educación de la Provincia de Buenos Aires (2017). *Resolución nro. 1664/2017*. RESFC-2017-GDEBA-DGCYE, Boletín Oficial PBA Nro. 28226, March 1, 2018

(2018a). *Resolución nro. 1107/2018. Educación inclusiva de niñas, niños,* adolescentes, jóvenes y adultos con discapacidad en la Provincia de Buenos Aires. RESFC-2018-1107-GDEBA- DGCYE, Boletín oficial PBA May 9, 2018.

(2018b). *Resolución nro. 4891/2018. Pautas para la certificación y titulación de estudiantes con discapacidad.* RESFC- 2018-4891-gdeba-dgcye, published December 18, 2018 in Boletín Oficial No. 28423.

(2019a). *Informe Evaluación Aprendizajes en Educación Especial, 2019* (retrieved May 5, 2020 from http://www.abc.gob.ar/informe-de-evaluacion- de-aprendizajes-en- educacion-especial)

(2019b). *2019: El estado de la escuela. Datos e indicadores* (retrieved July 1, 2020 from http://www.abc.gob.ar/sites/default/files/el_estado_de_la_ escuela_ ano_2019_1.pdf).

(2020). Resolución no. 33/2020 del 27/enero/2020, RESOC-2020- 33-GDEBA-DGCYE, Boletín oficial PBA January 31, 2020

Dirección General de Cultura y Educación de la Provincia de Buenos Aires & Grupo art. 24 por la Educación Inclusiva (2019*). Educación inclusiva y de calidad, un derecho de todos* approved by Resolución Nro. 6257/2019 (RESFC 6257-DGYE-19), Boletín oficial November 8, 2019 available as pdf at http://abc.gob.ar/sites/default/files/educacion_inclusiva_y_ de calidad_un_derecho_de_todos.pdf (consulted June 8, 2020) and Boletín Oficial de la Provincia de Buenos Aires November 22, 2019, https://www. eldial.com/nuevo/boletinBA/2019/BA191122.pdf approved by Resolution November 8, 2019, No. 6257/2019 (RESFC-2019-6257- GDEBA-DGCYE).

Edmund Rice International & Educación Inclusiva ONG (2017), *Comité de los derechos de las Personas con Discapacidad, 18va Sesión, Informe Conjunto* (retrieved September 16, 2020 from https:// tbinternet.ohchr.org/_layouts/15/treatybodyexternal/Downloa d.aspx?symbolno=INT%2fCRPD%2fICS%2fARG%2f29253&Lang= es)

Great Britain, Parliament (1981). *Education Act 1981* (retrieved June 9, 2020 from http://www.legislation.gov.uk/ukpga/1981/60/enacted)

Grupo Artículo 24 por la Educación Inclusiva (2017) *Informe Sombra ante el Comité de los Derechos de las Personas con Discapacidad, de la Organización de las Naciones Unidas* (retrieved September 16, 2020 from https://tbinternet.ohchr.org/_layouts/15/treatybodyexternal/Download. aspx?symbolno=INT%2fCRPD%2fICS%2fARG%2f284 78&Lang=es)

Instituto Nacional de Estadísticas y Censos (2010). *Censo Nacional de Población, Hogares y Viviendas 2010. Censo del Bicentenario.* Serie C. Población con dificultad o limitación permanente (2014). Buenos Aires. INDEC. Available at https://www.indec.gob.ar/ftp/cuadros/sociedad/ PDLP_10_14.pdf

(2019). Identificación de la población con discapacidad en Argentina: aprendizajes y desafíos hacia la ronda censal 2020. Documentos de Trabajo Indec Nro. 24. in *Aspectos conceptuales de los censos de población y vivienda: desafíos para la definición de contenidos incluyentes en la Ronda 2020.* - 1a ed. - INDEC, 2019. (Digital book, PDF available at https://www.indec. gob.ar/ftp/cuadros/publicaciones/discapacidad_ronda_censal_2020.pdf consulted July 9, 2020)

Province of Buenos Aires. Ley de Educación de la Provincia de Buenos Aires. Nro. 13.688 (2007). Passed July 5 2007; published July 10, 2007 Boletín Oficial PBA

Nro. 25692 (available at https://normas.gba.gob. ar/ar-b/ley/2007/13688/3181)

Ley del Estatuto Docente de la Provincia de Buenos Aires. Nro. 10.579 (1987) and amendments (available at http://www.abc.gov.ar/rrhh/sites/default/ files/ ley_10579_0.pdf)

Ley Nacional de Educación Nro. 26206 de la Nación Argentina (2006). Passed December 27, 2006, published in Boletín Oficial de la Nación December 28, 2006 and erratum February 6, 2007 (available at https://www.argentina.gob.ar/sites/ default/files/ley-de-educ-nac-58ac89392ea4c.pdf)

Ministerio de Educación y Deportes de la Nación Argentina (2017). *Guía de orientación para la aplicación de la resolución del Consejo Federal de Educación Nro. 311 del 15 de dic. de 2016*. Approved by Resolution No. 2509 -RES. MEyDN 2509/17- (retrieved July 3, 2020 from http://unterseccionalroca. org.ar/imagenes/ documentos/leg/Resolucion%202509-2017%20 (MEyD-%20Guia%20por%20 Res%20311-06).pdf
(2017). Resolución Nro. 2945 (RES. MEyDN 2945/17).

ONU (1945). *Carta orgánica de la Organización de las Naciones Unidas*, San Francisco, June 26, 1945 (available at https://www.un.org/es/ charter-united-nations/)
(1948). *Declaración Universal de los Derechos del Hombre*. Paris, December 10, 1948 (available at http://undocs.org/A/RES/217(III))

(1966). *Pacto Internacional de los Derechos Civiles y Políticos*. New York, December 16, 1966 (available at https://www.ohchr.org/SP/ Professional Interest/Pages/CCPR. aspx)

(1966). *Pacto Internacional de los Derechos Económicos, Sociales y Culturales*. New York, December 16, 1966 (available at https://www.ohchr. org/SP/Professional Interest/Pages/CESCR.asp x

(1989) *Convención sobre los Derechos del Niño*. New York, November 20, 1989, available at https://www.ohchr.org/SP/ProfessionalInterest/ Pages/CRC. aspx#:~:text=Art%C3%ADculo%201,antes%20la%20 mayor%C3%ADa% 20de%20edad)

(2006). *Convención sobre los Derechos de las Personas con Discapacidad*. New York, December 13, 2006, available at https://www.un.org/esa/ socdev/enable/ documents/tccconvs.pdf)
(2013). *Informe de la oficina del Alto Comisionado de las Naciones Unidas para los Derecho Humanos, Estudio temático sobre el derecho de las personas con discapacidad a la educación*, A/HRC/25/29, 2013

(2016) Comisión Revisora Derechos de las Personas con Discapacidad *Informe de cuestiones previas*. CRPD/C/ARG/QPR/2-3 (retrieved May 12, 2020 from https:// documents-dds-ny.un.org/doc/UNDOC/ GEN/G17/273/87/PDF/G1727387. pdf?OpenElement)

Organización de Estados Iberoamericanos para la Educación, la Ciencia y la Cultura (2010). *Metas educativas 2021: la educación que queremos para la generación de los bicentenarios*. Madrid: OEI

Organización Mundial de la Salud (2017). *10 datos sobre discapacidad* (retrieved September 16, 2020 from https://www.who.int/features/factfiles/ disability/es/s/)

Permanent Assembly for Human Rights, Users of Mental Health Assembly for Our Rights, Azul Association, Andar Civil Association, Críos Civil Association, Association for Equality and Justice, Colibrí Association, Association for the Support of Persons with Schizophrenia and their Families of the province of Jujuy, Association of Persons with Down Syndrome, Association for Civil Rights, Center for Legal and Social Studies, "Alicia Moreau" Center for Research and Teaching in Human Rights – National University of Mar del Plata, Commission for the Inclusion of Persons with Disabilities, University Commission on Disability- National University of La Plata, Argentine Federation of Institutions for the Blind and Visually Impaired, Argentine Federation of Rare Diseases, Federation of Protected Workshops, Despejarte.com Foundation, Integrando Foundation, Tigre Foundation for Inclusion, Tomar Acción Foundation, Rumbos Foundation, Specialized Institute on Disability Law of the Rosario Bar Association, Intersectional Working Group on Disability and Human Rights of Córdoba, Movement of the Blind and Visually Impaired Unit of Rosario, Observatory of Mental Health and Human Rights of Córdoba, Program of Disability and Human Rights – Faculty of Law – National University of Rosario, Network for the Rights of Persons with Disabilities (2018). *Committee on the rights of persons with disabilities. 18th Period of Sessions / Evaluation on Argentina. Status of persons with disability in Argentina 2013/2017.* (retrieved September 16, 2020 from https://tbinternet.ohchr.org/_layouts/15/treatybodyexternal/ Download. aspx?symbolno=INT%2fCRPD%2fICS%2fARG%2f285 78&Lang=es)

Red por los derechos de las personas con discapacidad -REDI- (2017), *Informe Alternativo: Situación de las personas con discapacidad en Argentina 2013/2017*, 18° Periodo de sesiones / Evaluación sobre Argentina, Comité sobre los derechos de las personas con discapacidad, ONU, available at http://www.redi.org.ar/ Documentos/Informes/Informe-alternativo- Argentina-2017/Informe-Alternativo-Argentina.pdf (consulted June 9, 2020)

UNESCO Educación Especial e Inclusión Educativa (2016). *XI y XII Jornadas de Cooperación Educativa con Iberoamérica sobre Educación Especial e Inclusión Educativa.* Organización de las Naciones Unidas para la Educación, la Ciencia y la Cultura and Oficina Regional de Educación para América Latina y el Caribe, OREALC/UNESCO Santiago (available at http:// www.unesco.org/new/fileadmin/ MULTIMEDIA/FIELD/Santia go/pdf/ XI-XII-jornadas-de-Cooperacion.pdf)

UNESCO (1990). *Conferencia mundial sobre Educación para Todos.* Jomtien (retrieved July 14, 2020 from https://unesdoc.unesco.org/ark:/48223/ pf0000184556)

(1994). *Declaración de Salamanca y marco de acción para las necesidades educativas especiales.* Conferencia mundial sobre necesidades educativas especiales: acceso y calidad. Salamanca, June 10, 1994 (retrieved June 5, 2020 from https://www.uniovedo.es/ONEO/wp-content/ uploads/2017/09/Declaraci%C3%B3n-Salamanca.pdf

Warnock Committee, Great Britain (1978). Special educational needs: The Warnock report. London. DES, at http://www.educationengland.org.uk/ documents/ warnock/warnock1978.html (consulted May 27, 2020)

World Health Organization & The World Bank (2011), World Report on Disability, available at https://www.who.int/publications/i/item/9789241564182)

10

ANNEX: QUESTIONNAIRE PROVIDED

Directorate-General for Culture and Education

DATA COLLECTION FOR DIAGNOSIS

Status of Situation of Inclusion of Students with Disabilities in the Education system of the Province of Buenos Aires

Preliminary Caveat: The information obtained from this survey will be used strictly for research purposes. There are no right or wrong answers; the basic aim is to assess the respondent's viewpoint.

The questions in no way and in no case refer to the performance of the respondent, but to their general view of the state/private schools in their region.

Personal information Questionnaire
(complete the form or circle the appropriate answer)

1	Age	1		
2	Sex	2		
3	Professional training (level and type)	3		
4	Job Position	4		
5	Length of service in the position	5		
6	Place of birth	6		
7	Level or modality	7		
8	State- or privately-run sector	8		
9	Have you ever had direct contact with a person with a disability?	9	YES	NO
10	Is there in your family a person with a disability?	10	YES	NO
11	Does any of your friends have a disability?	11	YES	NO
12	Does any of your coworkers have a disability?	12	YES	NO
13	Do you know any student in your district that has a disability?	13	YES	NO

Directorate-General for Culture and Education

Survey Questionnaire

Each respondent is asked to mark ONE of the options on the columns corresponding to each statement, always focusing on the present situation of the schools in their own regions/district/area.

The aim is to obtain information on the present status of inclusion of students with disabilities in the entire education system of the Province of Buenos Aires.[1]

Questions will be divided into 3 dimensions (CULTURES, POLICIES and PRACTICES), within which you will find 4 or 5 titles. Each heading will include 4 statements; the respondent should tick THE ONE option they think best reflects the reality of the schools in their region.

---

1 This questionnaire was adapted for this survey based on the methodologies generated by Mel Ainscow and Tony Booth in their book "Index for Inclusion. Developing learning and participation in schools" (2000) and by UNESCO in their document "A guide to ensuring inclusion and equity in education" (2017)

Directorate-General for Culture and Education

FIRST DIMENSION: CULTURES

1. Cooperation between personnel	Yes, in most schools	Yes, in some schools	In almost no schools	I lack information
a. Teachers and classroom assistants are involved in curriculum planning and revision				
b. There exists shared work between teachers in the classroom(two teachers in the same class				
c. Personnel know who to resort to with a problem, urgent or otherwise.				
d. Personnel have adopted as their own the school´s development plan.				

2. Relationship between school personnel and families	Yes, in most schools	Yes, in some schools	In almost no schools	I lack information
a. All families are thoroughly informed on education policies and practices.				
b. Families have room to get involved in decision-making about the school.				
c. A variety of occasions are provided where families can discuss their concerns and their children's progress.				
d. School staff value the knowledge that families have about their children Students are helped to have learning-, not result-geared objectives				

Directorate-General for Culture and Education

3. Relationship between school staff and members of the school co-operative	Yes, in most schools	Yes, in some schools	In almost no schools	I lack information
a. School staff and members of the school co-operative know one another.				
b. The capabilities and knowledge of the members of the School Co-operative are valued.				
c. The school's co-operative is fully informed about the educational center's policies.				
d. School staff and co-operative members share the approach concerning pupils with "special educational needs".				

4. Involvement of local institutions in the school	Yes, in most schools	Yes, in some schools	In almost no schools	I lack information
a. The center involves in its activities the various institutions of the area (local entities, associations, collectives)				
b. The members of local institutions share resources with personnel and students (library, classrooms, computers, etc.)				
c. All areas of local institutions are considered a resource for the center				
d. Local institutions have a positive opinion on the school				

5. Expectations concerning students	Yes, in most schools	Yes, in some schools	In almost no schools	I lack information
a. All students are treated as if there was no limit to their possible achievements				
b. Students´ achievements are valued in connection with their possibilities, instead of compared with other students´				
c. The use of student stereotypes through general labels is avoided, particularly in the case of students with learning difficulties or from different environments				
d. Students are helped to have learning-, not result-geared objectives				

6. Valuation of students	Yes, in most schools	Yes, in some schools	In almost no schools	I lack information
a. Students and staff with or without disabilities are valued alike				
b. The works of all students are exhibited in the center and its classrooms				
c. Efforts are made for report cards to be understandable for students and their family members				
d. All students complete the mandatory education cycle with an officially recognized diploma				

7. Elimination of obstacles to learning and participation	Yes, in most schools	Yes, in some schools	In almost no schools	I lack information
a. Personnel are aware of their potential capacity to prevent students' difficulties				
b. Obstacles to learning are considered to originate inside the organization itself, policies, curriculum, and teaching approaches as well as in the interaction of these aspects with students				
c. It is understood that labeling some students as having "special needs" might set them apart from other students of mainstream schools				
d. The teaching staff work in a cooperative manner (in teams or sharing the classroom) to introduce pedagogical improvements that enable all students to succeed				

8. Reduction of discriminatory practices	Yes, in most schools	Yes, in some schools	In almost no schools	I lack information
a. Personnel and students are aware that policies and practices should reflect the diversity of the school's students				
b. Personnel consider that disability arises when the person with impairments encounters negative attitudes and institutional obstacles				
c. Personnel try to counteract stereotyped attitudes towards persons with disabilities (e.g. that they cannot have a relationship, that they deserve compassion or that they are heroic fighters against adversity)				
d. The exclusion of students with severe disabilities is seen as the reflection of the existence of limitations in attitudes and policies rather than the result of practical difficulties				

Directorate-General for Culture and Education

9. Guiding principles of education policies, plans and practices	Yes, in most schools	Yes, in some schools	In almost no schools	I lack information
a. The national curriculum is based on principles of inclusion and equality, is solid and flexible enough to adapt to all students and is inspired by the social model of disability				
b. Current legislation is known, understood and put into practice by all teachers and managing team of the region				
c. The special education service provided in the province is sufficient and has a positive impact on the learning process of people with disabilities				
d. Access to clinical records and diagnosis of students with disabilities is imperative to ensure the provision of education service oriented to meeting their needs				

10. Appointment and promotion of staff	Yes, in most schools	Yes, in some schools	In almost no schools	I lack information
a. Promotion opportunities are open to all eligible persons, within and outside the school				
b. There exists a clear strategy to eliminate obstacles to the appointment of personnel with disabilities				
c. Specific sectors of the community are favored disproportionately when higher status positions are filled				
d. The fact that they value diversity of students is a bonus at the moment of personnel appointment				

11. Accessibility of schools	Yes, in most schools	Yes, in some schools	In almost no schools	I lack information
a. The needs of persons with hearing or visual impairments, be they total or partial, as well as the needs of persons with physical disabilities are taken into account at the time of making buildings and school spaces accessible				
b. Organizations of persons with disabilities are consulted, mainly on those aspects related to school accessibility				
c. Accessibility is considered the cornerstone of inclusion of all persons with disabilities, be they students, teaching and non-teaching staff, family members or the community at large				
d. The school makes sure it is knowledgeable about the existing legislation in the country concerning universal design and accessibility of persons with disabilities				

12. Support and assistance to new students as they adjust	Yes, in most schools	Yes, in some schools	In almost no schools	I lack information
a. The school has a welcome and integration program for students				
b. There exists available information concerning the education system in general and the school in particular				
c. The new student is clear about who to resort to in case of experiencing difficulties				
d. Measures have been put in place to facilitate transition between pre- and primary school, and between the latter and secondary school				

Directorate-General for Culture and Education

13. Organization of study/learning groups	Yes, in most schools	Yes, in some schools	In almost no schools	I lack information
a. Heterogeneity/diversity (of sex, capacities, interests,...) are the basic criteria to organize groups (courses)				
b. Efforts are made to reduce to a minimum the organization of groups according to levels of achievement, capacity or shortcomings of students				
c. Groups inside courses are sometimes reorganized to foster social cohesion				
d. The school avoids restricting the curriculum (e.g.: not taking into account a foreign language) for students receiving additional support in their process of literacy acquisition				

14. Activities of professional development of teachers and their connection with student diversity	Yes, in most schools	Yes, in some schools	In almost no schools	I lack information
a. Teachers are given the opportunity to observe and analyze their own classes and reflect upon them in connection with their students				
b. Personnel receive training concerning the development and management of cooperative learning activities				
c. Opportunities are created so that both personnel and students learn about peer-tutoring and coaching				
d. Teachers and other professional school staff learn to employ technology to support learning in the classroom (e.g.: cameras, videos, overhead projectors, computers, the Internet)				

15. Assessment of special education and support needs	Yes, in most schools	Yes, in some schools	In almost no schools	I lack information
a. External support services contribute to the planning and development of an inclusive type of teaching, geared towards the elimination of obstacles to learning and participation				
b. School professionals specify and agree with external support services a clear framework concerning how they should support learning within the educational center				
c. Individualized curricular adjustments serve to improve teaching and learning strategies for all students				
d. Assessment reports of students with "special educational needs" specify the support necessary to maximize their participation in the standard curriculum and in the community				

16. Disciplinary expulsion of students for behavioral reasons	Yes, in most schools	Yes, in some schools	In almost no schools	I lack information
a. Meetings are organized including personnel, students, parents and other members of the school community so as to approach problems in a flexible manner before they turn more serious.				
b. The responses of the school oriented to the improvement of students' behavior are geared towards education and comprehensive development of students rather than towards punishment				
c. Expulsion from the classroom is considered an extraordinary practice, always to be followed by the resuming of communication between student and teacher				
d. Clear reports are kept on formal and informal disciplinary expulsion of students for behavioral reasons				

Directorate-General for Culture and Education

17. School absenteeism	Yes, in most schools	Yes, in some schools	In almost no schools	I lack information
a. All obstacles to school attendance are analyzed in the school, as well as those connected with the attitude of students and their families				
b. The educational center refrains from using unexcused absences as a reason for disciplinary expulsion of students, as there exists awareness of the connections existing between unexcused absences, intimidation or maltreatment and social isolation				
c. There exists an effective system to keep a record of absenteeism and detect the underlying causes				
d. Records of absenteeism are a means to explore student/teacher relationships as well as relationship with the subject taught				

18. Class planning and development	Yes, in most schools	Yes, in some schools	In almost no schools	I lack information
a. Class methodology is adapted to respond to students´ various learning styles				
b. It is clear to the student what are the learning objectives of activities				
c. A variety of activities is employed, e.g. debate, oral presentation, writing, drawing, problem solving, use of the library, audio visual material, hands-on activities or the use of information technology				
d. Students have opportunities to carry out their assignments and express their knowledge in various ways, e.g.: expressing themselves in their mother tongue with translation/ interpretation, through drawings, photographs or a recording				

Directorate-General for Culture and Education

19. Accessibility of lessons	Yes, in most schools	Yes, in some schools	In almost no schools	I lack information
a. Special attention is paid to ensure all students have access to the oral and written language				
b. During lessons, the technical vocabulary corresponding to each program is explained and practiced				
c. Personnel recognize the physical efforts made by some students with disabilities or chronic illnesses to complete tasks, as well as the physical exertion entailed				
d. Through the use of alternative instruments in science classes or proposing differentiated physical activities in sports classes, teachers provide alternative modalities of access to the experience or understanding on the part of students that cannot take part in specific activities				

20. Evaluation of students	Yes, in most schools	Yes, in some schools	In almost no schools	I lack information
a. A variety of assessment strategies is employed to ensure all students can display their abilities				
b. Feedback is provided to students so that they can recognize what they have learnt and what they should do next				
c. Evaluation results are used to introduce changes in syllabus creation and teaching itself so as to adapt it to the needs detected				
d. A personalized report is produced reflecting in a positive manner the qualitative progress of students				

Directorate-General for Culture and Education

21. Support of learning and student participation	Yes, in most schools	Yes, in some schools	In almost no schools	I lack information
a. The objective of teachers is to make students as independent from direct support as possible				
b. Teachers seek alternatives to individual support, e.g.: through planning of classroom work and resources or group learning				
c. The presence of other adults (family members, teachers in training…) is considered an opportunity to reflect upon the curriculum and teaching methods for all students				
d. Efforts to eliminate obstacles to learning and participation of one student in particular are considered opportunities to improve the experience of all students				

22. Allocation of resources	Yes, in most schools	Yes, in some schools	In almost no schools	I lack information
a. It is clear how resources are allocated to support students of various ages and levels of learning				
b. Resources to respond to "special educational needs" are employed to boost the capacity of the school to address diversity				
c. Support resources are addressed at preventing obstacles to learning and participation and at reducing student labeling or categorization				
d. Staff regularly review the use of resources so that they can be employed in a flexible manner in response to the changing needs of the entire body of students				

Directorate-General for Culture and Education

23. Information and effective use of resources	Yes, in most schools	Yes, in some schools	In almost no schools	I lack information
a. There exists an updated record of the resources available in the area that can provide support to learning				
b. Members of local organizations contribute to the implementation and development of the education and curricular project of the school				
c. Members of the families and of the community are part of support resources in the classroom				
d. Adults with disabilities are involved in student support				

24. Level of experience of school personnel	Yes, in most schools	Yes, in some schools	In almost no schools	I lack information
a. Teachers are motivated to hone and share their abilities and knowledge to support learning and not only those aspects related to their personal job position				
b. Teachers with specific abilities and knowledge offer their help to others				
c. Personnel have both formal and informal opportunities to resort to everyone else's experience to address and solve issues and concerns relating to students				
d. Personnel of special educational centers in the area, if any, participate, share and interchange experiences with personnel of mainstream schools				

Directorate-General for Culture and Education

25. Student diversity	Yes, in most schools	Yes, in some schools	In almost no schools	I lack information
a. Students with a higher level of knowledge and abilities in one specific area sometimes play the role of tutors or mentors of other students				
b. Students of various ages are given the opportunity to support one another				
c. Each student is considered to possess important knowledge to teach others by virtue of their uniqueness, regardless of their level of achievement or capacity				
d. Obstacles to learning or participation of some students (e.g.: access and mobility within the premises or difficulties with a specific aspect of the curriculum) are used as problem-solving assignments or projects				

26. Teacher education and training	Yes, in most schools	Yes, in some schools	In almost no schools	I lack information
a. Teachers and support personnel get, during their initial training, the required tools to respond to student diversity				
b. Initial teacher training emphasizes the principle of inclusion				
c. Initial teacher training provides sufficient tools to implement the necessary support mechanisms to address disabilities in the classroom, at all levels and modalities				
d. Teachers of all levels and modalities have incentives to attend training activities regarding the approach in the classroom to disability				

Made in the USA
Columbia, SC
19 March 2025